Elton John

25 Years In The Charts

Elton John

25 Years In The Charts

John Tobler

HAMLYN

Editor: **Mike Evans**

Assistant Editor: **Michelle Pickering**

Production Controller: **Michelle Thomas**

Picture Research: **Wendy Gay, Anna Smith, Claire Gouldstone**

Art Editor: **Penny Stock**

Design & Art Direction: **David Palmer Design Practice**

First published in 1995 by Hamlyn,

an imprint of Reed Consumer Books Limited,

Michelin House, 81 Fulham Road,

London SW3 6RB

ISBN 0–600–58777–0

First published in Australia in 1995 by

CIS Cardigan Street Publishers,

245-249 Cardigan Street,

Carlton,

Victoria 3053

ISBN 1-86391-555-9

A catalogue record for this book is

available from the British Library

Printed in Hong Kong

Contents

			Page
Introduction:	Skyline Pigeon	1947 - 1969	6
Chapter One:	Your Song	1970 - 1971	16
Chapter Two:	Rocket Man	1972 - 1973	40
Chapter Three:	Don't Let The Sun Go Down On Me	1974 - 1976	68
Chapter Four:	Victim Of Love	1976 - 1980	100
Chapter Five:	I'm Still Standing	1981 - 1985	126
Chapter Six:	Sacrifice	1986 - 1990	146
Chapter Seven:	Made In England	1991 - 1995	176

Skyline Pigeon

Reginald Kenneth Dwight, now known throughout the world as Elton John, was born on March 25th, 1947, in Pinner, a northwest London suburb. His father, Stanley Dwight, was in the Royal Air Force at the time, prior to which he had been a trumpet player in a competent and quite well-known dance band, Bob Miller & The Millermen. His mother, Sheila (née Harris), had been working for the RAF as a clerk when she met Stanley. Even after the end of the Second World War, Stanley Dwight continued working in the armed forces, necessitating overseas postings which he undertook without his wife and child accompanying him. These kept him absent from home (Sheila's parents' house) for long periods, so that the young Reggie was effectively brought up by his mother and her family, and perhaps the major advantage he gained from his father was his musical ability, which, even when he was a child, enabled him to perform perfectly a piece of music after a single hearing. However, father and son also shared a passion for soccer in general, and the local league team, Watford FC, in particular. (In fact, there was a fairly famous footballer in the Dwight family, Stanley's nephew Roy Dwight, who had played for Fulham and later for Nottingham Forest.)

Piano lessons from the age of six (which by all accounts he enjoyed, unlike many children at that age) gave Elton a solid musical foundation, upon which he built by winning a part time scholarship to the Royal Academy of Music when he was still a pre-teen. This ensured that his grasp of musical theory balanced his inevitable obsession with the popular music of the time – Bill Haley, Elvis Presley, Jerry Lee Lewis, Little Richard and the other early rock'n'roll heroes. His mother, who had been a teenager during the war, was initially more interested in this exciting music than her son, who preferred the popular piano players of the time, including Liberace (whose flamboyance must have impressed the young music student) and Winifred Atwell, who had been born in Trinidad but moved to England where she accumulated over a dozen chart hits. However, before long the juvenile Reggie was more excited by piano pounders like the wild men of rock Jerry Lee Lewis and Little Richard – the young prodigy apparently saw Little Richard performing in a show at a local cinema, and was suitably awestruck.

Even as a child, Elton viewed his record collection as of prime importance in his life, spending hours not only listening to records but also relishing the sight and the feel of them, filing them carefully and never letting anyone borrow them in case they got scratched. When his parents divorced in the early 1960s, Elton almost certainly turned with even greater passion to his loved record collection, although Fred Farebrother, his mother's new partner who would later become

Bluesology

his step-father, displayed more interest in the adolescent boy than his natural father had shown. The new family moved a few miles to the north, to the very similar (if marginally more upmarket) suburb of Northwood Hills.

A public house known as the Northwood Hills Hotel was where the teenage Reg Dwight paid his dues as a performer, and it was Fred Farebrother who helped him acquire the job as pub pianist there. This involved not only playing current hits, such as the Ray Charles ballad 'I Can't Stop Loving You' and Bruce Channel's 'Hey Baby', but also singalong oldies, chestnuts like 'My Old Man Said "Follow The Van"' and 'Bye Bye Blackbird' – it was his task to play requests, and his natural ability and pleasant manner helped him achieve considerable local popularity within a few weeks. Still in his teens, he also joined a local R&B group, Bluesology, leaving school shortly before his GCE examinations – he felt he would hardly need qualifications other than talent to become a rock star.

Bluesology's original vocalist was Stuart Brown, who later fronted a progressive rock band known as Cochise in the early 1970s. Bluesology could not be deemed a successful act of the time, and although they released singles in 1965, '66 and '67, all failed to reach the chart. Interestingly, the major track on both the 1965 and 1966 releases was an original composition by Reg Dwight: 'Come Back Baby', the earlier single which also featured his first released vocal performance, and the later 'Mr Frantic'. Elton recalled: 'The first one was before we'd even turned professional, and in fact I sang on it, because it was too high for Stuart to sing. The second thing we did was a really diabolical thing called "Mr Frantic".'

Both can be judged musical milestones purely for historical reasons, and their commercial failure hardly affected Bluesology, who spent much of their time as a local backing band for visiting American R&B acts such as Billy Stewart and Patti LaBelle & Her Bluebells. By the time Bluesology turned professional in late 1965, Reg Dwight had left school, although only weeks before taking his 'A' level exam in music (which he would almost certainly have passed), but with four 'O' levels (including music) under his belt.

Perhaps Bluesology's lack of chart success was due to a repertoire inclining more towards jazz than up-to-the-minute R&B. Elton told me during an interview for *Zigzag* magazine circa 1971 at his Virginia Water house: 'Thinking we were a cut above the average club band, we were concentrating on things like "Times Are Getting Tougher Than Tough" by Jimmy Witherspoon, who was a sort of blues underground figure at the time.' Throughout the first part of the mid-1960s, via an introduction apparently arranged by Roy Dwight, his famous footballing relative, the 18 year old also worked as an office boy at Mills Music, a small music publishing concern in London's Tin Pan Alley, Denmark Street. Although hardly a first step on the ladder to success in the music business, it was certainly a foot in the door, and it was while he was making tea and running errands that he first encountered another teenager named Caleb Quaye, who worked in a similar capacity for another music publisher. When Elton's solo career began a year or two later, Quaye would be his first choice as lead guitarist on his records. When Bluesology reached the point where they were able to regard themselves as genuinely professional, working most nights and backing their heroes and heroines, Elton handed in his notice to Mills Music.

Unfortunately, their frustration at their failure to cut a hit led to the personnel of the band changing, with only Elton/Reg and Stuart Brown remaining of the original line-up. In late 1966, a short time after the group had spent a month in Hamburg playing at the celebrated Top Ten club where The Beatles had played a few years earlier, the Bluesology line-up included Reg Dwight, Stuart Brown, drummer Pete Gavin (later of Heads, Hands & Feet), Neil Hubbard on guitar (who went on to work with The Grease Band and Kokomo), bass player Freddy Gandy and a horn section of Marc Charig (trumpet) and Elton Dean (saxophone).

At the end of 1966, they were invited to become the permanent backing band behind Long John Baldry, a tall and distinguished looking vocalist who had worked with many big names in British R&B such as Alexis Korner, Cyril Davies and Brian Auger's Steampacket (with Julie Driscoll and a then unknown Rod Stewart). After Baldry had left Steampacket and was embarking on a solo career, he needed a backing group, a job he offered to Bluesology after seeing them perform at a London club, and one which they accepted with alacrity, although Reg Dwight, who had been the group's second singer (Stuart Brown was the main vocalist), initially found himself relegated to third in the vocal pecking order, and later was hardly allowed to sing at all when the American actress Marsha Hunt was also recruited to sing, a decision driven in no small measure by the idea that she improved the group's onstage image.

In late 1967, Baldry unexpectedly found himself at the top of the UK pop chart with a song which he had recorded with an orchestral backing, 'Let The Heartaches Begin', in which Bluesology were not involved, and, as Elton noted in our 1971 interview: 'Within a fortnight, Stuart and Marsha had left, because it obviously wasn't worth John's while to keep them, and we were playing big ballrooms – the high spot of our act being where Baldry used to sing his hit to a backing tape that we had to mime to. As Baldry's style changed towards the soft ballady stuff, we gradually moved into cabaret, and it was beginning to bring me down.' The B-side of Baldry's UK Number One when it was released in the US some time later was 'Lord You Made The Night Too Long', apparently one of the first records ever released in America with a songwriting credit to the team of Elton John & Bernie Taupin.

For some time, Reg had been thinking about a new job to replace the downwardly spiralling Bluesology, and an advertisement appeared in *New Musical Express* looking for 'talent' to work under the wing of the London office of Liberty Records, an American company which had just been launched as an independent label in Britain. The advert had been placed by a young talent scout named Ray Williams, who listened as the 20-year-old Reg Dwight sang a few oldies, accompanying himself on the office piano. Williams felt the voice was pleasant enough, and paid for Reggie to re-record the same songs in a professional studio so that they could be played to his American boss. When he asked whether Dwight had written any original songs, he was told that writing the music wasn't a problem (two of his songs had already appeared on Bluesology

Long John Baldry, circa 1964

DJM

singles), but that he lacked confidence in his ability to write lyrics. Williams also arranged an audition after which Elton was turned down both by Liberty Records and its music publishing arm, but Williams obviously felt the young musician should be encouraged, even if only in some small way. Williams had received numerous replies to his *NME* advertisement, and remembered one from a teenage lyricist who lived in Lincolnshire: Bernard Taupin. Perhaps the lyricist without melodies and the tunesmith without words could work together.

Bernie Taupin was born on May 22nd, 1950, and brought up on a farm. His father, Robert Taupin, worked in agriculture, and his mother Daphne (née Cort) was prevented from completing her education at university by the Second World War, and after her marriage became a farm worker's wife and mother to Bernie and his older brother Tony. When Bernie Taupin left school at the age of 15, he apparently had vague aspirations towards becoming a writer on a local news-paper, but ultimately ended up apprenticed in the printing trade, which was not really what he had in mind. However, he became extremely keen on listening to popular music, particularly the narrative country-flavoured ballads of Marty Robbins, and a little later the lyrically powerful work of Bob Dylan, finding it an escape from the mundane frustrations of labouring jobs, only under-taken to earn beer money.

Bernie also responded to the advertisement placed by Ray Williams. Williams must be cred-ited with engineering the original formation of a songwriting team which has earned similar success to that accorded other legendary duos like Lennon & McCartney, Leiber & Stoller, even Rodgers & Hammerstein. Williams was on good terms with the trio who fronted The Hollies, Graham Nash, Allan Clarke and Tony Hicks, who operated their own music pub-lishing company which rejoiced in the acronymic name of Gralto. Williams wanted a known publisher to administer the songs in which he had an interest, which were assigned to a company called Niraki, so any songs Elton wrote would be considered for publishing by Niraki. Gralto in their turn were administered by Dick James Music, and this was to be a most fortuitous chance alliance, probably the connection which triggered the entire Elton John success story.

Dick James' success peaked when he published the music of The Beatles, having signed them when no one else was interested. By the late '60s he had installed a small studio in the office block which was his HQ, in which songwriters whose work his company published could make demonstration tapes of their new creations. Whether this was because he foresaw the imminent rise of the singer/songwriter and wanted to encourage the writers already signed to his company, or that he had simply equipped the room to offer cheap studio time to expose raw tal-ent (which he could sign to his publishing empire) is irrelevant, because the studio (perhaps by mistake), was equipped for more than demo tapes, and was where Elton would eventually record his first solo album.

The coincidences which permeated the story of the rise and rise of Elton John and Bernie continued – the job of managing the studio was given to Caleb Quaye, the young guitarist who

Dick James, whose company published songs by both the Beatles and the Elton John/ Bernie Taupin team had worked as an office boy at the time Elton was running errands for Mills Music, and who had recently joined Dick James Music with specific studio responsibility. Elton would hang around the studio when he wasn't working with Bluesology, vaguely collaborating with two other young writers signed to Niraki, and sometimes playing keyboards for others who came in to use the facilities, including Clarke, Nash and Hicks and the songwriting team of Roger Greenaway & Roger Cook, who had two sizeable hits under their belts as vocalists using the alias of David & Jonathan, the first a cover of Lennon & McCartney's 'Michelle' and the second an original song they had written, 'Lovers Of The World Unite'. In 1969/70, Elton would play piano on several tracks released by The Hollies, including two notable hit singles, 'He Ain't Heavy, He's My Brother' and 'I Can't Tell The Bottom From The Top'.

At this point, Bernie Taupin and Reg Dwight had never met, although Elton had been sent a number of Bernie's lyrics which he would set to music. Bernie finally plucked up the courage to come to London to meet Ray Williams, who arranged for the future writing partners to meet. However, as Bernie was still based in Lincolnshire, early collaborations were undertaken by post; a lyric mailed from Lincoln would arrive in London, where it would be set to a tune then returned. Elton later recalled: 'I came up with one I quite liked called "Scarecrow", which I took along to Ray, who also liked it.' This has always been widely regarded as the first complete song written by Elton John & Bernie Taupin (although experts suggest that while it was certainly an early song, it was possibly the first one they felt they would admit they had written), and soon afterwards Dick James became aware of them, as Elton remembered: 'It was ridiculous how many people were making demos at Dick James' studio, but one day he discovered what was going on and had a big purge, finding out who was using his facilities. "Who the hell are Reg Dwight and Bernie Taupin?" he shouted, and he got Caleb to play some of the stuff we'd recorded. I don't think he was very impressed, but he agreed to sign us because Caleb, who was his blue-eyed boy, said he thought it was good. So we signed with Dick James as songwriters; he guaranteed us ten quid a week each, which was less than I was getting in the group, but it was all I needed, so I gave my notice in.'

Sheila Dwight recognisedthat the new partnership might stand a better chance of working if the geographical divide between her son and Bernie were eliminated, and Bernie was invited to stay in the Farebrother/Dwight residence. Around this time the first Elton John album was recorded, although it has never been released, and if Elton's memory of it remains the same today as in 1971, it probably never will: 'I was doing demos of the songs and we made them into an album, produced by Caleb on the two-track machine. There were songs on it like "Regimental Sergeant Zippo" and "Watching The Planes Go By", but of all the songs we wrote in that era, only a couple have ever seen the light of day – "The Tide Will Turn For Rebecca", a Johnny Mathis-type thing that Edward Woodward recorded, and "I Can't Go On Living Without You", which Dick James put in for the Eurovision Song Contest. It got to the last six in the year Lulu did the songs [1969], and Cilla Black subsequently recorded it.'

In 1967, Reg Dwight adopted his professional name, which appeared on his first solo single, 'I've Been Loving You'. This was released in the early spring of 1968 on Philips Records (via a licensing arrangement with Dick James Music), and had been produced by Caleb Quaye, but rather than using his own name, Elton decided to make a fresh start: 'It was obvious that Reg Dwight lacked the right sort of ring for a singer's name, so we decided to change it to Elton John – the Elton bit was pinched from Elton Dean, and John I got from our beloved Mr Baldry.' He added: 'The record was an Engelbert Humperdinck-type ballad which promptly died an abysmal death.' And fair to say, it provided no clue that he would become a superstar in a few years.

It was back to writing, and the brief excitement when a song was covered, released and flopped. The only exception to this depressing scenario was the team's first classic song, 'Skyline Pigeon', which was covered by Guy Darrell, whose version became a turntable hit, and also by Roger Cook. Solace from Elton's recording career was not forthcoming: 'I tried cutting a single produced by Zack Laurence [aka Mr Bloe] . . . a total failure, and then I cut a Mark London song, "Best Of Both Worlds" . . . another miserable failure.' Things were not going well: 'Caleb, who wanted to get on to other things, was having violent ructions with Dick James, who didn't want to know, so subsequently left. That meant that there was nobody at Dick James Music who was interested enough to help us.' Not only that, but Elton was having second thoughts about his long-term relationship with his fiancée, with whom he and Bernie Taupin were sharing a flat. Elton made an apparently 'theatrical' suicide attempt and, during a night out at a drinking club, Bernie and Long John Baldry persuaded him to back out of his scheduled wedding day. A few years later, that very same night on the town inspired Bernie to write 'Someone Saved My Life Tonight', one of Elton's most memorable hits from the semi-autobiographical album 'Captain Fantastic & The Brown Dirt Cowboy'.

Left
Bernie Taupin and Elton pose for an early DJM publicity shot, still with everything to prove

Below
An advertisement for Elton's first solo single, released in 1968

A change for the better for Elton & Bernie was inevitable, and came in the shape of Steve Brown, a DJM promotion man, whose job was to publicise and recommend songs which were published by the company. Brown, recognising the immense promise their songs displayed, instructed them to write what they wanted to write rather than songs in the style of a current hit or a successful artist, which had been their brief previously. For all the encouragement felt by Elton and Bernie when they signed to Dick James Music, they were regarded as little more than craftsmen, certainly not as artists. Elton was impressed by Brown: 'He said the fault lay in the fact that we were doing things half and half – partly as we wanted, but partly as Dick wanted, and it was coming out as a mish-mash. He told us to write what we wanted – which was an incredible thing to say really, because he was only a plugger for DJM.'

Below
Elton Dean, later a member of Soft Machine. Reg Dwight adopted part of his colleague's name when he conceived his stage name of Elton John

Brown assumed responsibility for the duo, encouraging them and criticising where appropriate, until they came up with a song he thought had potential, certainly for airplay and maybe even for the chart. Finally such a song appeared, Elton recorded it just before Christmas 1968 with Steve Brown as producer, and 'Lady Samantha' was released in the New Year. Elton reckoned he would always remember making that record: 'We hired an electric piano which was so abysmally out of tune that I had to play round a lot of notes.' He wasn't sure he wanted it to be released, but Brown was keen and, despite his misgivings, the single, which was again released on Philips through the DJM production deal, received so much radio play that many would have presumed it was a hit – but it wasn't. Even so, it was very encouraging, and according to Elton sold 20,000 copies – by no means a stiff. Perhaps most importantly, it finally convinced Dick

James that he wasn't wasting his time and money: 'Dick said that it was alright if we went ahead and made an LP, and though we'd prepared plenty of material which we wanted to record, we just couldn't believe it . . . an album all to ourselves.'

'Empty Sky' was Elton John's first LP, and was released in the UK in June 1969. The nine songs on the original album plus 'Lady Samantha' were recorded between December 1968 and April 1969, and produced by Steve Brown at Dick James Studios. The long title track was a slice of R&B reminiscent of something by Bluesology, with harmonica player Graham Vickery (aka Shakey Vick) guesting, while Elton played harpsichord on 'Val-Hala', a song featuring Taupin's mystic Viking mythology lyrics. 'Western Ford Gateway' was one of Bernie's numerous lyrics of that era about an America he had never seen. 'Hymn 2000' has typically cryptic Taupin lines – 'collecting submarine numbers on the main street of the sea' – and features session musician Don Fay playing flute. Most of the instrumentalists playing on the album were friends and acquaintances of either Elton or Steve Brown, such as Caleb Quaye on guitar and percussion, drummer Roger Pope and bass player Tony Murray.

On one track, 'Lady What's Tomorrow', Nigel Olsson, then working with Spencer Davis, was the drummer – he would later join Elton's touring band. The stand-out track on 'Empty Sky' was widely acknowledged to be 'Skyline Pigeon', again with Elton playing harpsichord – the song which had already been recorded by Guy Darrell and Roger Cook. It was re-recorded by Elton himself in 1972 during the recording sessions for 'Don't Shoot Me, I'm Only The Piano Player', and this later version reasonably enough featured him playing piano rather than harpsichord. The later version was released as the flipside of 'Daniel', an international hit single in 1973.

Even before the release of the 'Empty Sky' LP, a follow-up single to 'Lady Samantha' had been released, but once again failed to give Elton his chart debut. The tracks selected, 'It's Me That You Need' and 'Just Like Strange Rain', were recorded during the same period as the LP, although part of 'It's Me That You Need' was actually recorded at Olympic Studios. The 'Empty Sky' LP remained unreleased in the US until 1975, when Elton was an established superstar and, unsurprisingly, it reached the Top 10 of the Billboard album chart at that time, although it has yet to reach the album chart in Britain.

One reason may be its final track: the extraordinary medley of 'Gulliver', which is a genuine song; 'Hay Chewed', a jazzy instrumental whose title was a parody of The Beatles' 'Hey Jude'; and finally 'Reprise', with brief snatches of each of the earlier tracks on the LP. In 1969, it was an innovatory idea as the conclusion to the debut album of a promising performer. Twenty-five years later, much of this album is of greater historical interest than as a milestone in the saga of Elton John & Bernie Taupin. Elton's performance cannot be significantly faulted, although he has subsequently called the album 'naive'. However, he has also said: 'Making the "Empty Sky" album still holds the nicest memories for me, because it was the first, I suppose. We used to walk back from the sessions at about four in the morning and stay at the Salvation Army headquarters in Oxford Street. Steve Brown's dad used to run the place, and he used to live above it.'

Background
Elton in an early press shot after signing with Dick James Management. Circa 1968.

Background
The Salvation Army HQ on Oxford Street, London, where Elton and Bernie were based during the recording of the 'Empty Sky' LP

Undoubtedly, Elton and Bernie were pleased with their first LP, but unfortunately, the public in general were somewhat less ecstatic, but this was probably because relatively few knew of the album's existence and it sold around 2,000 copies. Steve Brown had also produced the follow-up single, 'It's Me That You Need', but after its unspectacular performance, he decided that what was really needed was a genuine producer.

Brown apparently decided not to beat about the bush and went straight to the top, offering the job to Beatle producer George Martin, but Martin would only consider the project if he could also write arrangements for the songs, which Brown had decided would benefit from orchestral backing. However, Brown had already chosen Paul Buckmaster (responsible for David Bowie's 'Space Oddity') as the right man for the arranger's job. When Buckmaster was asked who he would recommend as potential producer of the LP, he nominated Gus Dudgeon, who had not only produced 'Space Oddity' but had also worked as engineer or producer with such big names as Eric Clapton (in John Mayall's Bluesbreakers), The Strawbs and The Bonzo Dog Doo-Dah Band. With such a reputation, Dudgeon was cautious of working with an unknown act, but after hearing the demos of 'Your Song' and 'The King Must Die', which were likely to be included on the next LP, he accepted the assignment.

The second half of 1969 found Elton and Bernie continuing to write songs, encouraged not only by the release of 'Empty Sky' but also by the choice of one of their songs as a potential British entry in the Eurovision Song Contest, even though it was ultimately rejected in favour of the mind-numbing 'Boom Bang-A-Bang'. Elton had also discovered another means of earning extra cash, as a hired hand who could produce alternative versions of hits for budget-priced LPs with titles like 'Top Of The Pops Volume 13' and 'Chartbusters 9', and with sleeves invariably bearing a picture of a 'dolly bird', and which were sold in supermarkets and garages as a cheap way of acquiring a cross-section of the songs in the chart.

These cover versions were recorded at high speed and often without much finesse, but Elton's dues-paying days at the Northwood Hills Hotel had given him confidence in his ability to sing a wide variety of material, and he appeared anonymously on several such albums, which later became highly collectable by his fans, although almost the only place where they could be retrospectively found was in junk shops. In 1995, a small independent record company, rpm Records, went to the trouble of licensing a number of the tracks on which Elton had appeared and compiling a CD titled 'Reg Dwight's Piano Goes Pop', causing considerable interest among Elton's followers with versions of hits of 1969/70 like Stevie Wonder's 'Signed, Sealed, Delivered I'm Yours' and the Creedence Clearwater Revival's hits, 'Travellin' Band' and 'Up Around The Bend'. Today, these recordings are curios, although it is plainly Elton singing 'Spirit In The Sky' and pretending to be a Beach Boy for a cover version of 'Cottonfields', but they were but a mere side issue compared with the concern he, Bernie and Steve Brown felt when it became clear at the end of 1969 that Dick James would allow them only one more chance to produce that elusive hit album – or else the golden goose would become eggbound.

Bad Side Of *The Moon*

Elton John

Rock And Roll *Madonna*

Into The *Old Man's Shoe's*

Grey *Seal*

Your Song

Border *Song*

Take Me To *The Pilot*

I Need You *To Turn To*

First Episode *At Hienton*

Sixty *Years On*

Tumbleweed
Connection

Country *Comfort*

Burn Down *The Mission*

Where To Now *St Peter*

Ballad Of A *Well-known Gun*

Talking *Old Soldiers*

Friends

17-11-70

Honky Tonk *Woman*

11-17-70

Honey *Roll*

Can I Put *It On*

Amoreena

Love *Story*

Son *Of Your Father*

Rock Me *When He's Gone*

Let's Burn Down *The Cornfield*

Your Song

Your *Song*

Above
Elton John, circa 1970.

Left
Elton onstage for an outdoor show at London's Crystal Palace Bowl in July, 1971

Above
Gus Dudgeon, the producer who strongly contributed to Elton's international breakthrough

The 'Elton John' LP plus several other tracks released as singles, including 'Bad Side Of The Moon', 'Rock And Roll Madonna', 'Grey Seal' and 'Into The Old Man's Shoes', were recorded during January 1970 at Trident Studios in London, and marked the initial collaboration between Elton and producer Gus Dudgeon. Dudgeon and Steve Brown, who had produced Elton's previous album 'Empty Sky', had never met, but Brown decided that if this should turn out to be Elton's final chance, he at least should work with a producer who had both experience and sympathy for the songs. After George Martin turned down the job, Brown was uncertain who he should contact, until Paul Buckmaster suggested that Dudgeon might be the right man to nurture the embryonic star towards success. With his enviable track record, Dudgeon rarely agreed to work with anyone who was effectively unknown – the plus factors of Elton's near-hit with 'Lady Samantha' were counterbalanced by the negative aspects of the Eurovision song in 1969, although its failure to become the UK entry probably encouraged Dudgeon much more than if Elton and Bernie had written 'Boom Bang-A-Bang'. And of course there had been one previous album released which, although it didn't set the world on fire, had not been rubbished by the music press. When Dudgeon heard Elton's vocal and piano demo recordings of 'Your Song' and 'The King Must Die', he was convinced.

Dudgeon is one of only two record producers who between them have overseen over 90% of Elton's work, and Chris Thomas, despite being the current incumbent, didn't produce an Elton album until 'The Fox', released in 1981. It is hard to over-estimate Gus Dudgeon's contribution to the high quality of Elton's LPs, particularly those released before 'A Single Man' in 1978 – ten studio albums, two live LPs and several compilations, covering the period when Elton was arguably the most successful performer in the world. Dudgeon must have sensed that he was coming into contact with extraordinary talent, ambition and energy: the combination of his own expertise, the erratic brilliance of Paul Buckmaster, the interesting lyrics and memorable tunes which poured out of the prolific songwriting team, and (although he would only discover it later), a staggeringly excellent live performer, would become the key to success beyond everyone's wildest dreams.

The instantly notable track on the album was 'Your Song', which became Elton's first major single, reaching the Top 10 on both sides of the Atlantic, although surprisingly not until early 1971, almost a year after the LP's release. Equally surprisingly, it wasn't the first single taken from the album – 'Border Song' had been released in the spring of 1970 by DJM in Britain and by the tiny Congress label in America. All his previous recorded efforts had been designed to launch Elton in Britain, rather than in the US – his style was perceived

to be American, and this was perceived by DJM to be a deterrent to any success in the US; why would Americans be interested in a piano playing singer/songwriter from England, when there were plenty of highly rated home-grown examples?

Congress, a subsidiary of the giant MCA corporation, had released 'Lady Samantha' earlier in 1970, but with no more success than in Britain. According to Elton John biographer Philip Norman, MCA were more interested in another act signed to DJM, and Elton was effectively little more than a makeweight to flesh out a package deal. When the act which MCA preferred failed to make any impact, label boss Russ Regan suddenly began to take Elton a lot more seriously, and realised that the act he had taken almost on sufferance from DJM might have a chance after all. Having said that, he certainly didn't realise that Elton, who was being virtually handed to his company on a plate, would turn out to be the bargain of the millennium.

'Border Song' was swiftly withdrawn as a Congress single to be reissued a few months later by another MCA-controlled company, the higher profile Uni label, becoming Elton's first ever hit, although its chart life was brief and not particularly glorious – just over a month in the bottom quarter of the US Hot 100 without making any real impact. Its flipside, 'Bad Side Of The Moon', was recorded during the LP sessions but ultimately excluded from the album. The gospel-tinged 'Border Song' brought the duo its first genuinely gratifying cover version – Aretha Franklin's reading of 'Border Song' was a US Top 40 hit at the end of 1970, although by then Elton's own stature

Portrait of the artist as a young man – Elton John in 1970

had grown, from a minor cult figure at the start of the year to a mainstream prospect before Christmas. In 1989, Aretha and Elton would duet on a US Top 10 hit, 'Through The Storm', but when 'Lady Soul' cut 'Border Song' in 1970, she was the superstar and he was just the new boy. 'Border Song' was also recorded by Jose Feliciano and by Eric Clapton, who covered it on the 1991 tribute album to the songs of Elton & Bernie, 'Two Rooms', but it has never been a British hit single.

The second single from the 'Elton John' album was 'Your Song', which almost overnight took Elton from obscurity to stardom. He must have played it live more than any other song in his repertoire, although it was not a monster hit, merely Top 10 on both sides of the Atlantic. However, numerous cover versions (often by MoR acts like Andy Williams and Roger Whittaker) have been recorded subsequently, but only Elton himself has made it an American hit. It has been a hit three times in Britain, first for Elton himself in 1971, then for 'Philly soul' star Billy Paul in 1977, and most recently for Rod Stewart (again on the 'Two Rooms' tribute album) in 1992. Perhaps the greatest accolade paid to 'Your Song' came from John Lennon who, after hearing it, described Elton as: 'The first new thing that's happened since we [The Beatles] happened'.

Another famous song on the 'Elton John' LP was 'Take Me To The Pilot' – Elton's original version is a testimony to Leon Russell's considerable influence on his piano playing. Russell was regarded in the early 1970s as a genius, not only for his Machiavellian domination of Joe Cocker's 'Mad Dogs & Englishmen' tour and movie, but also for his participation in George Harrison's 'Concert For Bangla Desh' and his work with Bob Dylan, all of which

Aretha Franklin

Leon Russell

Border*Song*

would occur in the months following the recording of the 'Elton John' LP: thus Elton's admiration for Russell and his enjoyment of the latter's records was more an indication of his awareness of future trends in popular music than the result of any first-hand contact with Russell.

There is no doubt that 'Take Me To The Pilot' is lyrically obtuse, and Elton later admitted that he had never understood the song's lyrics, and also noted that Taupin didn't understand them either! The lyricist recalled hearing that David Bowie wrote songs by picking words out of a hat, and claimed that French avant-garde poets like Baudelaire and Rimbaud had used the same experimental technique because they wrote while under the influence of mind-expanding subtances and discovered the results could be pleasing, if less than straightforwardly comprehensible: 'It's how they sound together, you don't have to worry whether it rhymes or whether the meter's great.' He confessed that he would be delighted if someone could explain to him the meaning of 'Take Me To The Pilot'.

'Elton John' was Elton's breakthrough into the big time when it was released in April 1970. Although it didn't quite make it into the British Top 10 and had dropped out of the UK chart by the autumn, it was significant as his first album to reach the British chart and, perhaps more importantly, was his first LP to be released in the US. It took three months before it even entered the American chart (for reasons which will become clear), but once there, it featured in the *Billboard* Top 200 albums for almost a full year, peaking in 1971 in the Top 5.

This was an impressive performance for an album completed in a week and recorded live, including Elton's harpsichord on 'I Need You To Turn To', although he later complained that his singing sounded 'like a schoolboy'.

Another lyrically obscure song on the album is 'First Episode At Hienton', which seems to be about an encounter with what was presumably an old girlfriend of Bernie's named Valerie after they had not met for several years – Taupin was from Lincolnshire, a county in which there is a village near the city of Lincoln named Heighington, possibly spelt phonetically as Hienton, although Elton experts favour another Lincolnshire village, Hainton. The heavy orchestration of 'Sixty Years On' makes the track memorable for its musical weight as well as the song's quality, while 'The Greatest Discovery', a much more straightforward item about the birth of a baby brother, seemingly struck a chord with many.

Additional tracks which were recorded during the same sessions were mainly used as B-sides to singles, like 'Bad Side Of The Moon' (flipside of 'Border Song') and 'Into The Old Man's Shoes' (flipside of 'Your Song'), although a 45 released before 'Your Song' and after 'Border Song' featured two tracks which were both omitted from the LP, 'Rock And Roll Madonna' and 'Grey Seal' – because it failed to chart, the single became highly collectable when Elton achieved superstardom. Additionally, 'Grey Seal' was re-recorded in 1973 and included on the 'Goodbye Yellow Brick Road' album. Apart from Elton himself and the inevitable Caleb Quaye, many of the musicians who played on the 'Elton John' LP were session players – bass player Dave

Above
Elton on stage in the early '70s wearing a shirt with the words 'Grey Seal' on the collar

Left
Live at Crystal Palace, 1971

Background
Elton performing at Crystal
Palace, July 1971

Richmond had been a member of the Manfred Mann group when the latter released its flop debut single 'Why Should We Not?' and Terry Cox was drummer with the celebrated folk/jazz quintet, Pentangle. The half dozen backing vocalists included Tony Burrows (lead vocalist on the chart-topping 'Love Grows' by Edison Lighthouse), Madeline Bell and Elton's earlier acquaintance Roger Cook (both of whom were later vocalists with hitmakers Blue Mink), and Lesley Duncan.

Even before the 'Elton John' album had been released, the team had started recording a follow-up. If the breakthrough album had been closer to pop than rock, 'Tumbleweed Connection' would portray Elton in a more meaningful light and consolidate his status in Britain, particularly as it did not include any tracks which DJM in their wisdom considered suitable for release as singles. Because Britain and America reacted in different ways to its lack of a hit single, it was less of a step forward in the US than in the UK, although, like its eponymous predecessor, it was certified gold for sales of half a million units. Both albums have undoubtedly sold several million copies in the two and a half decades since they were first released, but as platinum awards were not introduced until 1976 (and multi-platinum certification was not adopted until 1984) estimates as to the precise status of either LP (probably double platinum or more) would be guesswork.

Perhaps the most telling aspect of the LP was how prolific the songwriting team of John & Taupin had become. 'Tumbleweed' was an important album for Elton, but by the time it had been released, he had made giant strides

in other areas. He had avoided live dates for the most part since leaving Bluesology, and could see little point in renewing his acquaintanceship with motorway travel. However, when Dick James (who had invested heavily in Elton) made it clear that he wanted Elton on the road to create a demand for his records, there was little alternative but to agree. James appointed his old chum Vic Lewis as Elton's agent, and Ray Williams, the talent scout who had initially engineered the collaboration between Elton and Bernie, joined DJM to become Elton's professional manager, as James himself could not afford to ignore his company's other profitable clients.

The next thing was to assemble a band of backing musicians. Fortunately, Elton was experienced and inventive enough to take responsibility for lead instrumental solo work himself, and Dick James would be pleased that he would only need to pay wages to a drummer and a bass player. The eventual rhythm section of the original Elton John Band (or Trio) comprised two musicians who were already connected with DJM – drummer Nigel Olsson had worked with Plastic Penny, who had included a song written by Elton & Bernie on a 1969 LP, while bass player Dee Murray (real name David Murray Oates) had been in an even more obscure combo known as Mirage. Olsson and Murray had worked together prior to this with The Spencer Davis Group (after the Winwood brothers had left the band in the late Sixties) so were by no means novices – it was no more than coincidental that the bass player on 'Empty Sky' also had the surname of Murray and his first name began with the same letter.

Nigel Olsson – drummer and original Elton John Band member, circa 1972

Dee Murray – bass player and original Elton John Band member, circa 1972

Jeff Beck – lead guitarist for The Yardbirds and later a solo star. Beck briefly rehearsed with the Elton John Band

It would be some time before the group expanded to a quartet with the addition of a lead guitarist, but it only became widely known some years later that the expansion came close to happening in 1970. Jeff Beck, who had been on the biggest hits by The Yardbirds and had then formed a new group featuring a then little-known Rod Stewart as vocalist (and future Rolling Stone Ron Wood on bass), was looking for a new band: 'I went through managers like a dose of salts at that time, and one of them put me on to Elton, and took me to The Speakeasy to see him play, but nothing happened immediately. A couple of weeks later, this manager persisted about us getting together, and said that he thought he could get Elton's drummer and bass player out, and Cozy [Powell, the drummer who worked with Beck] and I and a great bass player. So we went for a rehearsal at Hampstead Town Hall, but I turned up late and he gave me a terrible roasting – it actually wasn't my fault because my car had broken down – and here I was playing guitar for a band that was already complete, because Elton didn't want to change his rhythm section. I thought the next thing would be he'd have me wearing a tie or something . . .'

Elton had a slightly different version: 'I always said I'd never mention this, but Jeff Beck came to talk to me after I'd done a set at The Speakeasy one night. He said he'd really like to join the band. Well, I obviously wasn't going to let an offer like that go by, but at the same time I was a bit worried that he may try to turn us into a wailing guitar group, which I was always against. Anyway, we set up rehearsals and I just simply couldn't believe how well Jeff fitted into the band, he was so good. But the crunch came when Jeff said: "I don't really like your drummer too much – I'd like to bring Cozy in." Well, we had a big meeting and I decided I'd rather just keep Nigel and Dee, because we'd only been going for a short time and I was really enjoying it.' Having spoken to both Elton and Jeff Beck, a personal feeling is that two such dominant personalities in the same band would have been little more than a recipe for excess, so perhaps it is as well that these titans did no more than rehearse together.

'Tumbleweed Connection' was the point where Elton began making inroads in Britain as a serious rock artist, an album act. The 'Elton John' LP had given confusing signals, especially with 'Your Song' following a Eurovision candidate and 'Lady Samantha', but when it was released in October 1970 'Tumbleweed Connection' was his first UK Top 10 LP, remaining in the chart for five months (several weeks longer than the 'Elton John' album). If this rock (as opposed to pop) image and direction was indeed the intention, it was somewhat diluted by the release in early 1971 of 'Your Song' as a single, which became his first UK chart 45, although confusingly it was not from his then newest and current LP. However, it seems unlikely that anyone felt disappointed when Elton finally achieved a chart breakthrough, whatever the declared intention beforehand. Oddly enough, when 'Your Song' was released as a single in America, it was the flipside of 'Take Me To The Pilot', but disc jockeys seemed to prefer it, so it became a hit there at the end of 1970, two months before it made the UK chart.

Tumbleweed
Connection

Many of the songs on the new album, which was again recorded at Trident Studios and produced by Gus Dudgeon, seemed to reflect Bernie Taupin's preoccupation and fascination with the American West and its accoutrements – outlaws, sheriffs, the great outdoors and the cowboy/soldier legend. Two of the album's ten songs included the word 'gun' in their title, and the sepia-dominated sleeve design reinforced the impression created by song titles such as 'Country Comfort', 'Burn Down The Mission' and 'Ballad Of A Well-known Gun'.

Nevertheless, not one song on this plainly great LP has ever been a chart hit for Elton, although a couple have been subsequently covered by other major artists.

'Ballad Of A Well-Known Gun', which on the 'Tumbleweed' original features Caleb Quaye's guitar punctuation and backing vocals by a six-strong choir including Dusty Springfield, Lesley Duncan, Madeline Bell and Tony Burrows, was recorded by James Taylor's younger sister Kate and included on her sole US chart album, and as she clearly lacked her big brother's self-confidence (as a songwriter) she also covered 'Country Comfort' on the same LP. This song has also been recorded by a bona fide country singer, Juice Newton, whose version appeared on her first hit album in 1981. However, it is probably best known, especially in Britain, because Rod Stewart included a worthy version on his second LP 'Gasoline Alley'. Elton's original version, which is arranged in a country-tinged style akin to bluegrass with guest players on fiddle (veteran jazzman Johnny Van Derek), pedal steel guitar (Gordon Huntley, another veteran who played with Matthews Southern Comfort) and harmonica (Ian Duck, the vocalist and front man of Hookfoot, Elton's DJM label-mates). The rest of Hookfoot – guitarist Quaye, drummer Roger Pope and bassman Dave Glover – all individually appear on parts of the album.

The final track, 'Burn Down The Mission', a stand-out stage stormer for Elton, is curiously like a precursor of latterday Gothic epics by Jim Steinman such as Meat Loaf's epic 'Bat Out Of Hell', in structure more than in lyrical content (though both use religious imagery). Were Elton & Bernie influential on Steinman? 'Mission' was covered by Phil Collins on 'Two Rooms', the 1991 tribute album of Elton & Bernie's songs, and Sting covered 'Come Down In Time' on the same all-star collection. One of the exceptions to the Western concept of the album, the latter is a modern romantic song with the sound of a harp (played by the memorably-named Skaila Kanga), and an oboe. It was also covered by both Judy Collins and Al Kooper, two critical favourites of the 1970s.

If two of the songs on 'Tumbleweed' dwell on morbid subjects, the compositional quality of both seems inspired. The universal dilemma of 'Where To Now, St Peter?', the agnostic concern about one's destination – heaven or hell – makes the song one of

Right
Guitarist Caleb Quaye who played on many of Elton's early albums

Far right
Dusty Springfield, herself a big star, who helped out as one of the backing vocalists on 'Tumbleweed Connection'

Below
Bernie Taupin, circa 1971

Taupin's most astute early lyrics. The more resigned 'Talking Old Soldiers' (a conversation between ex-comrades) is dedicated to 'David' (identified in Philip Norman's *Elton – The Definitive Biography*, as American singer/songwriter David Ackles). In 1972, Bernie Taupin would produce 'American Gothic', the third album by Ackles, and this collaboration was probably first mooted when Ackles was the opening act for Elton's first live appearances in the US at the famous Troubadour club in Los Angeles in August 1970, which was where Elton's career in America was launched and went swiftly into orbit.

He recalled: 'We'd been offered a gig at The Troubadour in Los Angeles and various other gigs in the USA, and I was going to cancel them to rehearse with Jeff [until he pulled his bombshell], but looking back, I think Jeff maybe wanted to take the band over and go touring the States on his reputation. I've got no malice towards him, in fact I think he's a really great guy, as well as being an incredible guitarist, but as I said, I told him no and that was it – we went off to the States on our own and it worked out fine. Jeff asked me not to tell anyone about it, but I don't suppose he's bothered any more, he's with those guys from Cactus now, so I imagine he's happy enough.'

The 'guys from Cactus' were bass player Tim Bogert and drummer Carmine Appice, known for their work as the rhythm section of Vanilla Fudge, the ultra-heavy hard rock sensation of 1968. The much-anticipated supergroup of Beck, Bogert & Appice made one studio album and another live effort released only in Japan, where it was recorded. Beck's rejection of a series of vocalists on the

grounds that they were not as good as Rod Stewart led to internal disagreements, not helped by the fact that two managers were involved based on opposite sides of the Atlantic Ocean.

Elton continued: 'I think the start of all the success was the Troubadour thing – it was just amazing. It's an incredibly funky little place, the best club of its kind anywhere, and all it is is some wooden tables and chairs and good acoustics. It only seats about 200, and the first night we played there it was packed to the brim with people from the record industry, who expected me to come on with this 15-piece orchestra and reproduce the sound of the album, which had recently been released there. We'd flown to Los Angeles, 13 hours over the pole in this jumbo jet, and we arrived to find this bloody great bus – "Elton John has arrived" and all that sort of thing – and it took another two hours to get to the hotel. Once we'd booked in, we were hustled out again and off to The Troubadour where The Dillards were appearing; they were incredible, just knocked me out.'

Elton's London agent, Vic Lewis, had managed to set up a club tour by reminding the owner of The Troubadour that the club had enjoyed success with another British act he had sold them, Pentangle, and had also promised that the club would be packed with celebrities (not difficult with someone as well-liked as David Ackles – once critics were at the club, it wasn't hard to keep them a couple of hours longer). Elton was inspired and for a week performed for the rock aristocracy, including Leon Russell, which freaked Elton out completely.

Left
Elton backstage at the Crystal Palace outdoor show, July 1971

By the time Elton and the rest of the party reached New York six weeks later, the 'Elton John' LP was in the US Top 20. He had to return to reality and to London to do a film soundtrack, 'Friends', which he'd contracted to do earlier in the year, as replacement for Ritchie Havens, who had been the first choice of the film company. However, the film turned out to be something of a disaster. This was not destined to be Elton's finest hour but the album would not appear until well into 1971.

Meanwhile, Elton had been invited back to the US for another tour, which included a show which would be transmitted live on American radio, using a recording studio with an invited audience. Elton described what happened: 'During our second tour of the States, which was mostly co-headlining with people like Leon Russell, The Byrds, Poco, The Kinks and so on, we were asked if we'd like to do a live broadcast. This hadn't been done in New York for years, and the radio station said it could be done in a studio, sent out in stereo, and that the sound would be really good. We played in headphones, and it all came out of this little recording studio which had an audience of about a hundred to create the concert hall atmosphere. We didn't know at the time, but afterwards we found that Steve Brown had arranged for an 8-track recording to be made – just to see how it came out – and when we listened to it, we thought it was quite good. The "Friends" album, over which we had no control, was about to come out, so we did a quick mix of the live recording at DJM and released an album from the tapes. At the time, I thought it was good enough, and I also wanted it to

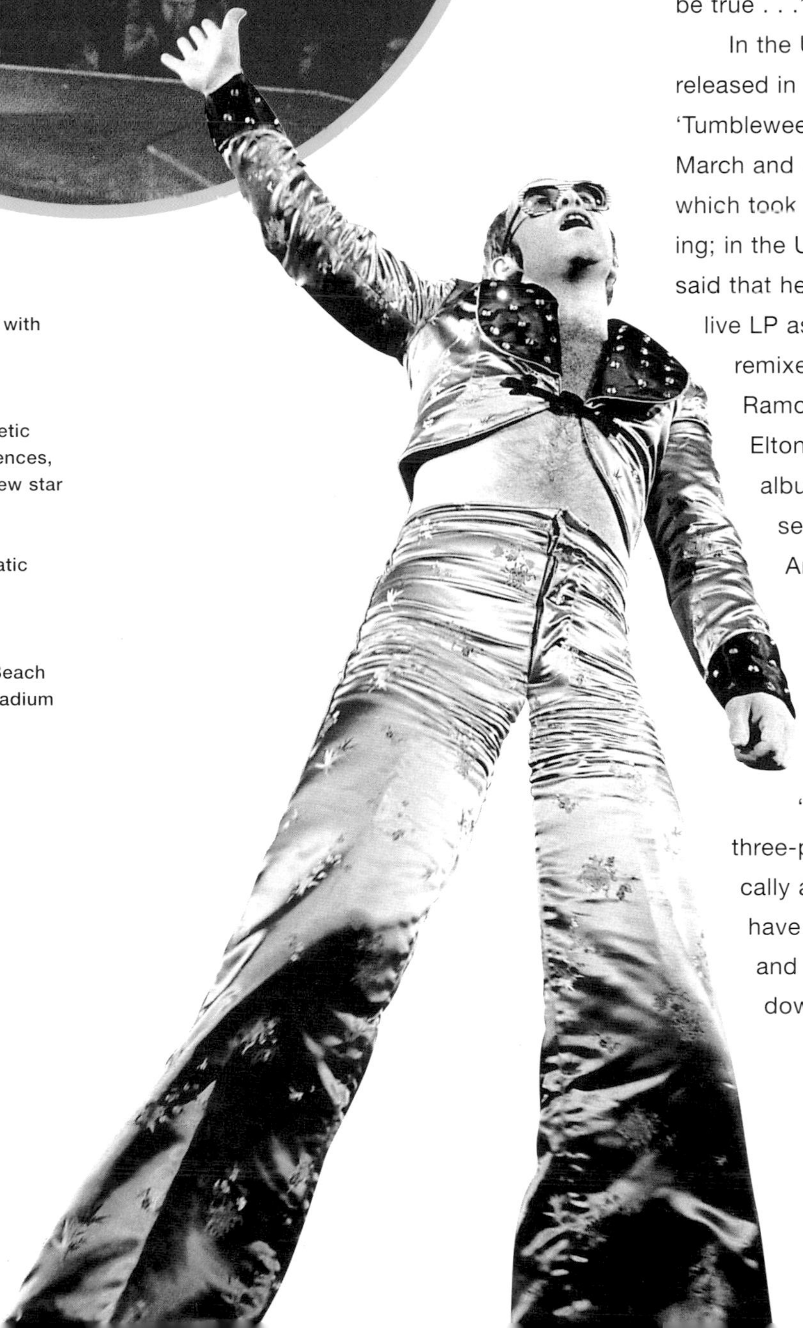

come out because Dee and Nigel, who had
been on very little before, were featured very
strongly. Looking back, it's not a wonderful
recording, but I think it's valid, despite the fact
that saleswise it was a disaster. Even "Empty
Sky" has outsold that one in Britain, and in
America, it only did 325,000 compared with
the previous two which both did over a million.
But it did mean that I had four albums in the
US Top 40, which hadn't been done since The
Beatles. The "Friends" album was officially
certified as gold, but I don't believe that can
be true . . .'

In the US, three new Elton John LPs were
released in less than six months –
'Tumbleweed' at the start of 1971, 'Friends' in
March and in May, '11-17-70' (the live LP
which took its title from the date of the recording; in the UK, it was titled '17-11-70'). Elton
said that he regarded the US version of the
live LP as superior, because it had been
remixed by American studio star Phil
Ramone at Trident Studios in London.
Elton also noted: 'I agree that the live
album is not very good,' and this
seems partly due to the repertoire.
An opening 'Take Me To The Pilot' is
received like the Second Coming,
and Elton is obliged to adopt a
Goon-like voice to say: 'Stop it, I
tell you, stop it.' How to maintain the frenzy? Start a cover of
'Honky Tonk Woman' *a capella* with
three-part harmonies, play it enthusiastically and end it as Leon Russell might
have done with a breakneck final chorus
and a climactic crescendo. Slow it
down with 'Sixty Years On' but without

Left
Elton on *Top Of The Pops* with
Mark Bolan, 1971

Above
Elton's reputation for athletic
stage antics wowed audiences,
who flocked to see this new star

Right
Elton acknowledges ecstatic
applause, circa 1971

Previous page
Elton on stage with The Beach
Boys at Crystal Palace Stadium
in 1971

the original's strings, and then plug the forth-coming 'Friends' soundtrack LP with 'Can I Put You On', which mentions all sorts of places in Britain and is perhaps the best thing on the movie album, but is really not classic Elton. Side Two, plug the last single, 'Bad Side Of The Moon' (the live LP was recorded ten days before 'Your Song' was released as a single, which presumably explains its absence from the album). Finally, the rabble-rousing 'Burn Down The Mission' cleverly arranged to incorporate a verse each from the early Presley side 'My Baby Left Me' and The Beatles' 'Get Back'. Was it lack of self-confidence which impelled him to include on the broadcast songs associated with arguably the three biggest names in rock? It must be admitted that the historical value of the live LP was somewhat greater than its entertainment quotient after a couple of plays, but it is by no means a poor effort.

That description (poor) is more appropriate when considering the 'Friends' soundtrack LP. Elton and Bernie had completed two songs, 'Honey Roll' and 'Can I Put You On', even before the deal was made for them to write the soundtrack music, and these two tracks feature Dee Murray and Nigel Olsson plus Caleb Quaye on guitar and a sax player. Gus Dudgeon produced the LP at Trident, and Paul Buckmaster was involved as arranger and composer of a few songs. Elton said: 'Lewis and John Gilbert taught us a lot about film music, and showed Buckmaster what it was all about.' Neither 'Friends' nor the live LP sold as well as either 'Elton John' or 'Tumbleweed Connection' in America, although both reached the Top 40 of the

Billboard chart, and 'Friends' was certified gold, although Elton suggested that the US record label, Paramount, had probably shipped sufficient copies for gold certification, but had not mentioned that many thousands of albums had been returned unsold.

Statistics suggest he may be absolutely right, as 'Friends' remained in the US chart for under five months and only made the Top 40, yet was certified gold, while '11-17-70' was there for nearly six months and all but reached the Top 10, but didn't go gold. In Britain, the live LP charted for two weeks, just making the Top 20, but 'Friends' didn't chart at all. Probably the major encouragement was that DJM had released 'Your Song' as a single in Britain and it was a Top 10 hit (his first in his own country).

The other excitement for Bernie Taupin was that he had become engaged to Maxine Feibelman, whom he had met on the first visit to Los Angeles to play The Troubadour. Maxine and Bernie thereafter had become inseparable and, as she was adept and skilled at sewing, she carried out running repairs to stage clothes. The couple were married in early 1971 in Lincolnshire, with Elton as best man, as the avalanche of EJ albums started. Fortunately for everyone concerned, the inspired 'Tumbleweed Connection' was established in the LP chart before the two less notable albums appeared. Critics and fans alike guessed – wrongly – that the lyrics on the LP showed how impressed Bernie Taupin had been by seeing America at first hand, but it transpired that the songs had been written before Bernie had been to the States, and he credited The Band's 'Music From Big Pink'

Elton flanked by Gary Glitter (left) and Rod Stewart (right)

album (and Robbie Robertson's songs) as a major influence, also noting that his earliest songwriting inspiration was Marty Robbins, an American superstar of country music, who did not neglect the cowboy tradition in country music with his platinum album of the late 1950s, 'Gunfighter Ballads And Trail Songs', and whose hits included 'Devil Woman' and particularly 'El Paso' which, Taupin felt, 'married rhythms and the printed word perfectly'.

The album's acceptance and popularity must have seemed to Bernie confirmation that he and Elton had also got it right.

'Amoreena', a regretful love song on which Elton was backed by Dee Murray and Nigel Olsson on record for the first time, is also the name of Elton's god-daughter, while 'Love Story' is an 'outside' song, written by Lesley Duncan, who plays acoustic guitar and duets with Elton on the track. 'Son Of Your Father' is the hugely cinematic but somewhat

Elton live! Edmonton Sundown Theatre, North London, 1971.

noir story of two brothers, one of whom is blind and has a hook instead of a hand. Much of the album seems so lyrically vivid that it is easy to imagine characters and places in a way that could inspire a film script. 'Tumbleweed' was almost a 'concept' album and may well have alerted The Eagles to the possibility of an album like 'Desperado', which treated similar subject matter in a conceptual fashion a year or two later.

Both Rod Stewart and Long John Baldry entered Elton's life again in 1971 and 1972 – Baldry's career had gone into deep decline, not helped by 'Let The Heartaches Begin' which, although it topped the UK chart, was light years away from his R&B roots. By 1971, Elton was well on the way to international fame, and Rod Stewart was also making major strides in similar directions, but Baldry was a forgotten man. In an attempt to revive his flagging fortunes, the two pupils-turned-stars

agreed to help him make a new LP, adding weight to his endeavours by sharing the production of the album.

Side Two, produced by Elton, included a new song he and Bernie had specially written, 'Rock Me When He's Gone', and which Elton recorded himself during the sessions for 'Madman Across The Water', although his version was only released officially in the 1990s. Elton's side of the album, on which he and Hookfoot worked as a backing band, also included a Randy Newman song, 'Let's Burn Down The Cornfield', but it seems that those who even recall the LP, which was titled 'It Ain't Easy', tended to concentrate on the side produced by Rod Stewart, which also featured Ronnie Wood (then Stewart's colleague in The Faces), Ray Jackson of Newcastle group Lindisfarne on mandolin and vocalist Maggie Bell of Stone The Crows. In sales terms, the project was a failure, although the media awareness of Baldry increased.

In 1972, Elton and Rod decided to try again, each producing one side of 'Everything Stops For Tea', which boasted a memorable sleeve portraying Lewis Carroll's Alice and the Rabbit at the Mad Hatter's Tea Party. Baldry was the Mad Hatter, of course . . . This time, no John/Taupin song was included, although Davey Johnstone appears on every track, Nigel Olsson on four of the five and Ray Cooper on a couple – Elton adds 'vocal accompaniment' to four of the tracks, but is not credited as an instrumentalist. This LP was no more successful than 'It Ain't Easy', and during the 1970s Baldry emigrated to Canada, where he is still recording and is seemingly better appreciated.

At the end of 1971, Elton was a megastar in America and little more than a contender in Great Britain, where Marc Bolan and Led Zeppelin shared the main limelight with Simon & Garfunkel. While his status in the US has hardly altered in the intervening two decades, it remains marginally above his British rating as merely a legend.

As if infected by the general euphoria, Bernie Taupin was invited to make an album of his own, reciting his poems against a musical backing produced by Gus Dudgeon. This was never likely to become a chart success, and it surprised no one when it was soon forgotten, although had Elton's name been featured in some way on the album sleeve perhaps things would have been different but, according to Philip Norman's book, Bernie would not allow his partner to appear on the record and in fact the only mention of Elton was in the use of his 'John' surname on the songwriting credit to 'The Greatest Discovery', which Elton had recorded himself on the breakthrough 'Elton John' release.

Apart from that sole namecheck, Elton John's name was conspicuous by its absence, although there were plenty of other names (and photographs) of people connected with Elton appearing on the sleeve. Gus Dudgeon produced the album and among the musicians who provided the backing were Caleb Quaye, Davey Johnstone and keyboard player Diana Lewis, while Steve Brown co-ordinated the project. Other musicians included Texas-born guitarist Shawn Phillips who also played sitar and had worked with Donovan, Richard Coff on violin and viola, percussionist Chris Karan, and bass player Ron Chesterman (an early

Left
Another flight captured at the Edmonton Sundown show, 1971

member of The Strawbs). The musicians were beyond reproach, with both Johnstone and Shawn Phillips playing guitar, sitar and other stringed instruments, but 'Taupin' (as the LP was titled) had almost nothing to do with songs and Bernie certainly didn't try to sing – this was a so-called 'poetry album', such as was vaguely fashionable in the late Sixties, with similarly trendy Indian-influenced music, although in fairness, it wasn't all sitars and Bernie's recitations.

The complete first side of the album was a series of poems under the collective title of 'Child', comprising 'The Greatest Discovery' and eight other parts including 'Flatters (A Beginning)' on which Davey Johnstone plays banjo, and 'Brothers Together', with Johnstone providing Celtic influence on mandolin. There is little here for Elton John fans other than those complete obsessives who must own every record with which he has even the most tenuous connection, though tracks like 'To A Grandfather' (a poem seemingly written after an elderly relative's burial) possess a certain dignified poignancy. While 'Taupin' was far from a total disaster, there was little public outcry when no follow-up album emerged. When he did resume his recording career, almost everything had significantly changed for Taupin – and everyone else. 'Taupin' must be regarded as a curio, from its faintly disturbing sleeve photograph of Bernie apparently clutching a lighted candle which has deposited hot wax on his fingers (although it has somehow failed to adhere to his wrist watch) to the small 20-page booklet inside the sleeve which contains the words to the 17 poems featured on the LP.

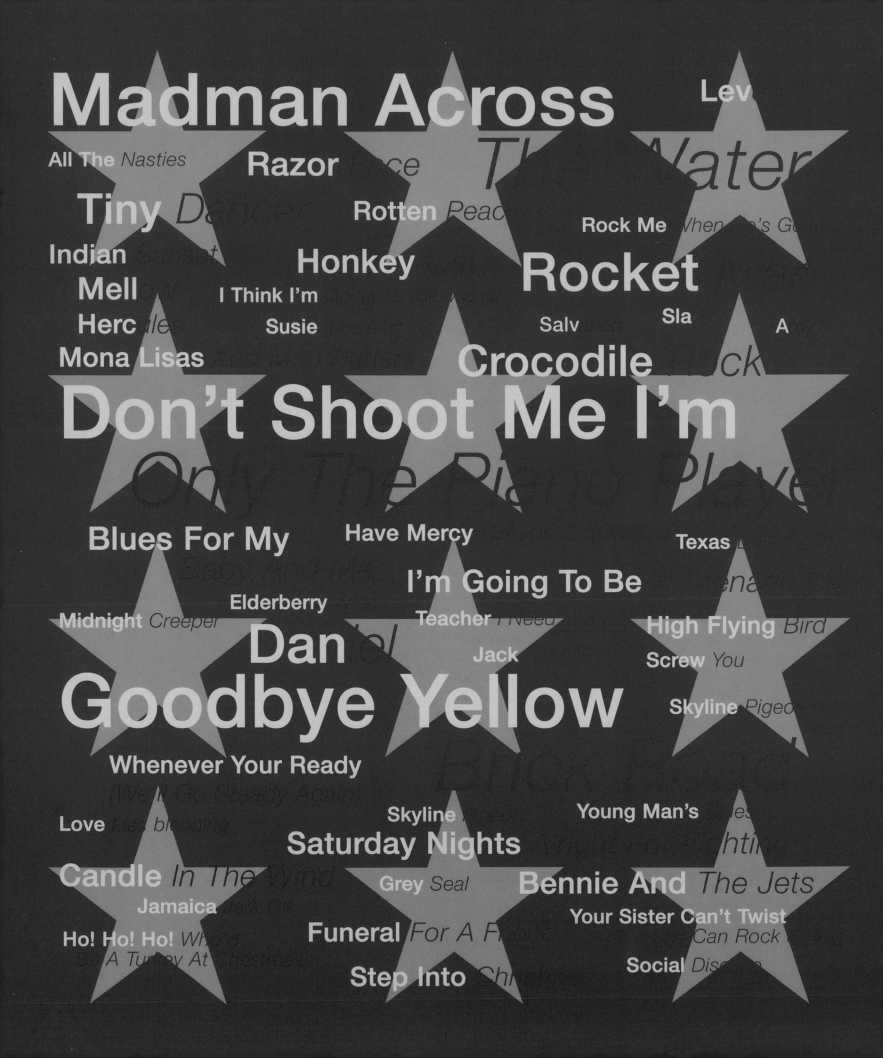

1972

Rocket *Man*

1973

Rocket**Man**

Above
Elton wearing one of his more outrageous costumes, 1972

Left
Elton with John Reid (left) and Gus Dudgeon (right) at the launch of Rocket Records, 1973

By the start of 1972, a new and significant member of the Elton John team had been introduced in the shape of John Reid, a young Scotsman who worked for EMI Records and, although young in years, was running the famous Tamla Motown label in the UK. This was considerable responsibility for one so inexperienced, as Motown's roster included Smokey Robinson, Diana Ross, Marvin Gaye and Stevie Wonder, not to mention The Temptations, The Four Tops and others. Elton, a genuinely obsessive record collector, had apparently inveigled himself with the label manager for Bell Records, another American company whose releases were handled by EMI in Great Britain, and a visitation would occur when the grapevine brought news of an interesting new release. Elton soon added John Reid to his EMI itinerary, because he adored Motown music. A friendship quickly developed leading to the urbane Scotsman and the singer/songwriter, who was a super-star in America but only a contender in Britain, sharing a flat in London's West End.

Above
(l.to r.) Stephen James, Bernie
Taupin, Elton, Dick James

Right
Elton on stage, 1972

Davey Johnstone

At this point, Dick James and Ray Williams
had fallen out badly enough for Williams to be
muscled out of Elton's career, but who could
replace him? How about the guy he shares a
flat with? Of course, we'll hire him to work for
DJM with special responsibility for Elton –
which turned out to be a decision James
would live to regret. Reid was exactly what
Elton wanted and, as it turned out, exactly
what DJM didn't want. It has been said that a
good manager spends all his time thinking of
how to enhance his client's career and to
organise every aspect of his life (within reason). Ray Williams had been far more involved
in the music biz than either Elton or Bernie
when he introduced them to each other and,
when he had rejoined Elton after the hiatus,
had somehow overlooked the fact that he was
now an employee and Elton was effectively
paying his salary.

Williams later said that Elton needed a
different type of manager, like the one he
ended up with, John Reid. After a time, Reid's
influence on Elton was far greater than that
wielded by Dick James, for whom Reid
worked. For Elton, there was no hesitation in
preferring his flatmate's opinion to that of Dick
James in decision-making, as both James and
his son Stephen had far less in common with
Elton. Reid encouraged Elton to make his own
decisions, and is still Elton's partner, manager
and friend nearly 25 years later. Dick James
came from the pre-rock'n'roll generation, and
simply unable to appreciate Elton's priorities
sympathetically, while Stephen James was the
right age to empathise with Elton but sided
with his father when differences of opinion
occurred. Reid was on the same wavelength

as Elton in many respects, while Stephen was
tuned in to the music biz establishment rather
than contemporary rock culture, to which
Elton was strongly attached.

There was another newcomer from
Scotland, Davey Johnstone, a fair-haired
young prodigy who played both electric and
acoustic guitar as well as banjo and mandolin.
Since the Jeff Beck episode, and even before,
Elton had longed for another instrumentalist
who could share the burden of solos – he himself was already lead vocalist as well as piano
player, and a solo in every song was getting
predictable to say the least. The obvious
choice as guitarist would have been Caleb
Quaye, but after Johnstone's work on
'Madman Across The Water', when he almost
effortlessly proved his potential by playing
exactly what was required on four tracks of
the LP, he got the job, no doubt assisted by a
recommendation from Gus Dudgeon.

'Madman Across The Water', released in
November 1971, was Elton's first studio LP of
that year, during the first half of which he had
released both the live album and the 'Friends'
film soundtrack, which included at least two
songs originally destined for the new studio
album. 'Madman' seemed to some to be a
reversion to the introspective singer/song-
writer style of 'Empty Sky', and while there is
some truth in that description, it is probably
Elton's most undervalued LP, certainly of the
early years of his career, perhaps because, like
'Tumbleweed Connection', it lacked major singles. However, both 'Levon' and 'Tiny Dancer'
were US hits, although neither reached the
Top 20, and Elton had no UK singles released
in 1971 at all. Even so, the LP reached the US

Top 10, stayed in the *Billboard* Top 200 for virtually a whole year (three months longer than 'Tumbleweed' and exactly the same number of weeks as the 'Elton John' LP), and became Elton's third gold album.

In contrast, 'Madman' was also Elton's least successful UK album (in chart terms) of those he made during the period when he was signed to DJM, with the exception of the 'Empty Sky' debut, which was released when he was a virtual unknown, and 'Friends', which surprised few when it also failed to chart.

The 'Madman' album was misunderstood when it was first released; it was the fifth new Elton John LP released in 18 months (April 1970 to October 1971), and there was an inevitable risk of overkill with what amounted to a new LP every three and a half months! Even now, over 20 years later too few people, especially in Britain, seem to realise what they have been missing.

What is interesting is that when these tracks were recorded in 1971 (several months after the live album), it was decided that Elton's recently acquired and eventually long-serving rhythm section of Dee Murray (bass) and Nigel Olsson (drums) should only play on a single track, the gospel-flavoured 'All The Nasties'. The other tracks featured session players and/or musicians from other groups, such as DJM label-mates Hookfoot, whose rhythm section of drummer Roger Pope and bass player Dave Glover, as well as Elton's chum guitarist Caleb Quaye, each perform on several tracks.

Among the songs on which they appear are the stunning opener, 'Tiny Dancer', which was dedicated to and inspired by Bernie

Taupin's wife, Maxine Feibelman, which also features British pedal steel guru B J Cole. They also appear on the contagious 'Razor Face', which additionally involves Rick Wakeman on organ and Jack Emblow on accordion, and 'Holiday Inn', on which Davey Johnstone excels on mandolin.

'Tiny Dancer' was the second US single from the album, and it all but reached the Top 40 soon after 'Levon' peaked in the Top 30. 'Levon' is certainly cinematic in its description of an individual who 'wears his war wound like a crown' and 'calls his child Jesus because he likes the name' – the name Jesus actually appears in three songs on the album: 'Tiny Dancer' ('Jesus freaks out in the street handing tickets out for God'), 'Levon' (as a Christian name) and 'Rotten Peaches' (an appeal to the almighty from a slave or an escaped prisoner), although this is probably coincidental. The latter track boasts Rick Wakeman and guitarist Chris Spedding, plus Pentangle drummer Terry Cox, Herbie Flowers on bass, Davey Johnstone on acoustic guitar and Diana Lewis on synthesiser. By contrast, the last track on the LP, 'Goodbye', features Elton alone. Cox and Flowers are also on the rather poetic 'Indian Sunset', which Elton starts *a capella*, and whose lyrics mention Geronimo.

Originally, it was probably overlooked in comparison with 'Tiny Dancer' and 'Levon', but the album's title track has more recently justified the considerable accolade of being its flagship song, not least by being covered by Bruce Hornsby on the 'Two Rooms' tribute album. Hornsby credits Elton with inspiring him to learn to play the piano and noted that

Rick Wakeman

he liked the song's 'dark mood'. Taupin has commented that the 'Madman' title track was misinterpreted more than many of his songs, and the subject of the song was widely pre-sumed to be the disgraced President Nixon post-Watergate. Interestingly, he offered no alternative explanation.

The original title track version has the same all-star cast as 'Rotten Peaches', and the song has become part of Elton's latterday concert repertoire. An early recording of the song was undertaken during the sessions which produced the 'Tumbleweed Connection' LP, and featured Mick Ronson on guitar rather than Chris Spedding – Ronson came to promi-nence around this time (early 1970s) as David Bowie's right-hand man in The Spiders From Mars, the 'Ziggy Stardust' band. Another acoustic version featuring folk guitarist Michael Chapman has also been mentioned, but the recording which includes Ronson was only released officially in 1991 on the 'Rare Masters' compilation. The celebrity-packed 'Two Rooms' also includes another song from the 'Madman Across The Water' album, 'Levon', covered by Jon Bon Jovi who said he wished he had written the song himself.

Around 20 other musicians accompany Elton on the various tracks on the 'Madman' album, and to these should be added ten backing vocalists who all appear on 'Tiny Dancer', 'Holiday Inn' and 'Rotten Peaches': Lesley Duncan (whose 'Love Song' composi-tion was included on the 'Tumbleweed Connection' album), Sue (Glover) & Sunny (Leslie), Barry St John, Liza Strike, Roger Cook, Tony Burrows, Terry Steele, Dee Murray and Nigel Olsson. In addition, both 'All The

Nasties' and 'Indian Sunset' feature the Cantores in Ecclesia choir, directed by Robert Kirby. The album was effectively recorded in two bursts – a couple of tracks on February 27th 1971, and the other seven between August 9th and August 14th the same year. The considerable activity which surrounded Elton and Bernie during that year resulted in only one track being recorded which was not used on the original LP, 'Rock Me When He's Gone', which, until the release of 'Rare Masters' in the early 1990s, had never been available on a legally released album, although it at one time existed in both demo and live versions on bootlegs.

After the frantic activity of 1971, during which he had released four new LPs in the US, there was time to draw breath during the six months after 'Madman' and before 'Honky Chateau', released in May 1972. The latter was Elton's first LP to top the US chart, hold-ing off all comers for five weeks during the summer, and was his first to remain in the *Billboard* Top 200 albums chart for well over a year. In the UK it was his first Top 3 LP, and not only included his first Top 3 single, 'Rocket Man', but was also his first album to include more than one hit single – the second UK chart item, which peaked just outside the Top 30, was 'Honky Cat'. In the US, both 'Rocket Man' and 'Honky Cat' were Top 10 singles.

'Honky Chateau' was also notable as Elton's first studio album recorded away from London (although the live LP had been taped in New York). The story goes that Elton had been strongly advised that considerable tax advantages would accrue from using a studio in another country, and while he would later

Mick Ronson

base himself in Britain and ignore such advice, in early 1972 (after the commercial disappointment in the UK of 'Madman Across The Water', a gold Top 10 album in the USA), he seemingly felt less loyalty to his own country, where he was merely a contender, than to the United States, where he was already a sensation and his popularity was still increasing.

The Rolling Stones were spending a year as tax exiles in France in 1971/2, and had announced their intention of recording their next album in France using a mobile studio. If it was good enough for the Stones (a group Elton had admired for many years), it was good enough for him. However, a suitable mobile studio could not be found, but Gus Dudgeon saved the day by suggesting a conventional studio which operated in a chateau built over three hundred years ago, which had been used by The Grateful Dead. Provided the studio equipment was technically acceptable, the Chateau d'Hierouville was an extremely viable alternative, especially as it was within easy reach of Paris (conveniently only 25 miles to the north of the French capital), while everyone involved with the recording could also live there, working all day and night if necessary, and for relaxation could enjoy the facilities offered by the private swimming pool and tennis court in the grounds. In addition, the food was highly regarded and the chateau had a vineyard of its own. With such advantages, it was difficult to object to Dudgeon's radical and exciting suggestion.

The finished album's title not only referred to Strawberry Studios (as it was known), but the LP was dedicated to Catherine Phillipe-Gerard, the chateau's manageress.

The recording studio at the Chateau d'Hierouville, 1971

Interestingly, the album basically involved just the quartet of Elton, Dee Murray, Nigel Olsson and Davey Johnstone. The few additional musicians included a horn section composed of French musicians little known in mainstream musical circles; jazz violin star Jean-Luc Ponty (who is also from France, and worked with Frank Zappa); 'Legs' Larry Smith (drummer of the eccentric Bonzo Dog Doo-Dah Band, who contributed tap dancing to the surprisingly cheerful 'I Think I'm mGoing To Kill Myself'); David Hentschel, whose synthesiser noises are a memorable aspect of 'Rocket Man', the track for which the album is probably best-remembered; and the almost inevitable Ray Cooper on percussion, plus a team of backing singers, the latter contributing the neo-gospel vocal sound to 'Salvation', a track in the vein of Delaney & Bonnie or Joe Cocker's giant 'Mad Dogs & Englishmen' project. 'Honky Cat', an amusing pun on the album's title, was a lively five-minute opener with its oriental piano intro and R&B horn section (arranged by Gus Dudgeon) and with Johnstone on banjo, while 'Mellow' was Leon Russell-ish, with Ponty's wailing electric violin. 'I Think I'm Going To Kill Myself', with its rather jaunty arrangement, was reminiscent of the ironic late Sixties classics by The Kinks, and 'Susie (Dramas)', with its contagious chorus, boasts a psychedelic guitar solo from Johnstone.

Then comes 'Rocket Man', with the truly memorable couplet 'Mars ain't no place to raise your kids. In fact, it's cold as hell', and those synthesiser swoops. It was deservedly a huge hit, and its chances could only have been improved by the fact that there had recently been a space launch (seemingly far

Honky*Chateau*

Above
The Chateau d'Hierouville where Elton recorded the LP 'Honky Chateau'. The recording studio was situated on the second floor indicated in the top left circle

Top right circle
Elton's bedroom in the Chateau

Bottom right circle
The studio desk on which 'Honky Chateau' was recorded

Above
Harry H Corbett, Wilfred
Brambell and Hercules the Horse
from the hit television series,
'*Steptoe And Son*'

Far Right
Elton at the dress rehearsal
for the Royal Variety
Performance, 1972

Right
French violin star Jean-Luc
Ponty

less notable in the Nineties than the way such
intrepid voyages were regarded two decades
ago). More importantly, it was Elton's second
hit single in Britain, where none of his last four
LPs had spawned a chart single, although it
was his sixth single to chart in the US.

The track remains instantly recognisable
as one of his most familiar hits. 'Slave' is
almost epic, with the final line of each verse
atmospherically repeated, and seems to be a
polite stylistic nod to The Band (who had
backed Bob Dylan, released seminal albums in
their own right, and were among Elton and
Bernie's favourite groups), with Davey
Johnstone's guitar and banjo reinforcing the
similarity, while 'Amy', on which Jean-Luc
Ponty is again featured, is like Leon Russell at
his most extreme.

A track which has been remembered
more vividly than some of its fellows is the
ingeniously titled 'Mona Lisas And Mad
Hatters', without drums and with Johnstone
on mandolin. This powerful and unromantic
reflection of Bernie Taupin's impressions of

New York tends to provoke community singing
when Elton performs it in concert. In contrast,
the echoed vocals of the closing 'Hercules'
feature both Fifties doo-wop passages and
late Sixties Beach Boys harmonies, and some
may be amused to learn that the song is about
a rhinoceros of that name. Elton's first country
residence in Virginia Water was also called
Hercules, perhaps another polite tribute, this
time not to fellow musicians but to the
Steptoe And Son TV series starring Wilfred
Brambell and Harry H Corbett, which Elton
enjoyed, and which included an ironically-
named horse the Steptoes called Hercules;
additionally, when Reg Dwight changed his
name by deed poll in December 1971, he
became Elton Hercules John.

'Honky Chateau' was a significant release
for Elton. It was recorded during January
1972, and was the first of three albums
recorded at the chateau, all of which topped
the US charts. It would seem that few notable
cover versions were made of the songs on the
album, with the obvious exception of 'Rocket
Man', the contribution by Kate Bush to the
1991 all-star tribute album of Elton & Bernie's
songs, 'Two Rooms'. For once, few of the
tracks recorded during the sessions were
omitted from the LP, but two have since
appeared: an alternate version of 'Slave' and
the rarely heard cover of the familiar Tommy
Tucker rhythm and blues classic, 'Hi-Heel
Sneakers'. Undoubtedly a milestone album,
this was Elton's first to reach the ultimate
plateau in pop music, the pole position in the
Billboard chart.

At the end of the year, Elton was invited
to perform before the Queen and Prince Philip

in the Royal Variety Show at the London Palladium on a bill which also included Liberace, whom Elton admired intemperately and in terms of showmanship seems to have been a piano-playing role model in his mastery of many styles. Elton played his new single, 'Crocodile Rock', which had only been released three days before.

'Crocodile Rock', a celebratory tribute to the 1950s, was a huge hit on both sides of the Atlantic, especially in the US where it became his first ever Number One single. It was included on 'Don't Shoot Me, I'm Only The Piano Player', Elton John's sixth studio LP and his eighth original album overall. Released in January 1973, it was his first to top the UK LP chart, remaining at Number One for six weeks, and his second US chart-topping LP during a chart residency of well over a year and a half. Surprisingly, it was Elton's first LP to include two Top 5 UK hit singles; in the US, it not only included his very first Number One single, but also a second 45 which reached the Top 3.

It was Elton's second album recorded in France, and it was appropriate, in the judgement of those around Elton, to return there for 'Don't Shoot Me'. The album was so titled, according to Philip Norman's book *Elton – The Definitive Biography*, after an off-the-cuff answer by Elton to a jocular accusation by the great comedian Groucho Marx, whom Elton met in Hollywood. The legendary veteran reckoned Elton's name was back-to-front, and that his parents were probably a Mr & Mrs Elton, who had called their son John. The gleamingly laminated album sleeve acknowledges Groucho's influence – the front cover shot is of the marquee above the street entrance to a

cinema, proclaiming that the main feature is *Don't Shoot Me, I'm Only The Piano Player* starring Elton John, while a smaller poster advertises an elderly Marx Brothers movie masterpiece, *Go West*.

The two huge hits so dominated the LP that many of the other tracks seem to have been unjustly ignored, such as 'Blues For My Baby And Me', a heavily orchestrated epic with a fine wah-wah guitar solo from Davey Johnstone, and with flourishes near the end recalling 'Forever Changes', the highly rated 1967 LP by Los Angeles group Love. 'Have Mercy On The Criminal' is another impressive song, which includes a riff closely related to Eric Clapton's famous 'Layla', while overall the song is similar in structure to 'Burn Down The Mission' from the 'Tumbleweed Connection' album. Love and Eric Clapton were yet more street-credible influences, and another, although in the country music area, was superstar Merle Haggard. 'Texas Love Song' may have been inspired by Haggard, and may even be a tribute to the reformed criminal who

Below
The flamboyant Liberace at the Royal Variety Show, London Palladium, October 1972

Right/Far Right
Elton alone (right) and with his band (far right) rehearsing for the 1972 Royal Variety Show

Merle Haggard

Centre
Elton with Marc Bolan and Ringo
Starr at the premier of *Born To
Boogie*

Right – insert
Elton (right) and Bernie (inset) at
the premier of *Born To Boogie*

Pevious page
Elton signs copies of his latest
LP 'Don't Shoot Me I'm Only The
Piano Player' in the Noel
Edmonds Record Shop on the
Kings Road, Chelsea, London,
January 20th, 1973

was pardoned after serving his time by the then Governor of California Ronald Reagan; Merle Haggard's significance was confirmed by his peers when he was elected to the Country Music Hall Of Fame in 1994.

'I'm Going To Be A Teenage Idol' was inspired by the meteoric success of Marc Bolan & T.Rex, who were as popular in the early 1970s as are Take That in the mid-1990s. While it could have been about any other teenage idol, Elton and Bolan were friends – they were both born in 1947 – and in fact Elton appeared as special guest in the concert based feature movie about Bolan *Born To Boogie*, which was filmed by erstwhile Beatle Ringo Starr. Philip Norman's book quoted Bernie Taupin as regarding Bolan as a minor talent, whose self-confidence was rather endearing.

The brassy R&B on 'Teenage Idol', the James Brown-like 'Midnight Creeper' and 'Elderberry Wine' (the B-side of the million-selling international chart-topper 'Crocodile Rock') were provided by the same quartet of French horn players who had contributed to the previous 'Honky Chateau' album: Jacques Bolognesi on trombone, Ivan Jullien (trumpet) and two saxophonists, Jean-Louis Chautemps and Alain Hatot.

Both 'Teacher I Need You' (a cross between Cliff Richard's 'Schoolboy Crush' and the Johnny Mathis hit 'Teacher Teacher') and

'High Flying Bird' (perhaps a nod to Davey Johnstone's folk roots) apparently resulted from a real effort by Elton to add variety to his vocals – the self-confessed vocal influences included such diverse figures as Van Morrison (on 'High Flying Bird') and Bobby Vee (on 'Teacher I Need You').

The LP as a whole includes many highlights, but none so commercially successful as 'Crocodile Rock', a nostalgic evocation of the late 1950s with a perfectly appropriate and instantly obvious steal from Pat Boone's 1962 novelty hit, 'Speedy Gonzales'. It was Elton's first million seller, and he admitted that it was 'derivative', but it was a huge hit, becoming his third single release to reach the British Top 10. This was soon to be followed early in 1973 by the rather more reflective and melodic 'Daniel', a second gigantic international hit within six months, which made the Top 5 in Great Britain and the Top 3 in the United States.

In the companion book to the 'Two Rooms' tribute album in 1991, Bernie Taupin confessed that the song had been inspired by an article in *Newsweek* magazine about Vietnam veterans: he felt the song was important because it was, he said, 'the one thing I said about the Vietnam war', although he also felt it was the most misinterpreted song he and Elton have written.

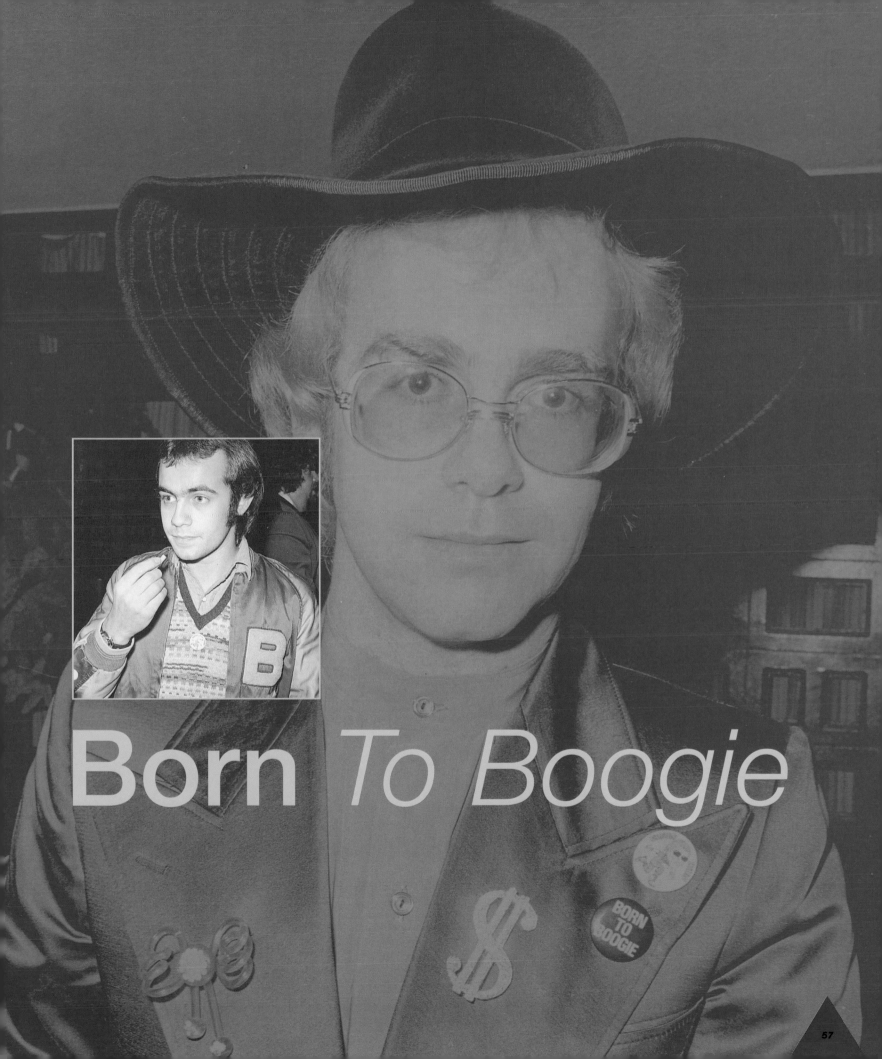

Born *To Boogie*

'Daniel' also includes synthesiser parts played by Ken Scott, who engineered the recordings for the first two albums made by Elton at the Chateau, but was hardly surprisingly not available for the next (and last) LP Elton made there – Scott also produced (rather than engineered) three notable albums for David Bowie, 'Hunky Dory', 'Ziggy Stardust' and 'Pin-Ups' in 1972/3, and perhaps understandably felt that as a fully fledged hit producer, it would be retrogressive to return to being instructed by Dudgeon (for whom he undoubtedly had great respect).

While Scott acquits himself well enough on synth, 'Daniel' wasn't quite another 'Rocket Man' (although its chart performance bettered that of the anthem of the lonely astronaut). Although he had intended to find an alternative studio for his next album, recognising some technical shortcomings at the chateau, the travelling Elton show would return there in mid-1973 to record the next (double) LP, 'Goodbye Yellow Brick Road'. Also recorded during the 'Don't Shoot Me' sessions was a new version of an early favourite from the John/Taupin repertoire, 'Skyline Pigeon', which had first appeared on Elton's debut LP, 'Empty Sky', in 1969, and was widely regarded as that album's major highlight. The new version, with piano instead of harpsichord, was not on 'Don't Shoot Me', but was released as the flipside to the single of 'Daniel'.

Three months after 'Don't Shoot Me' was released, Rocket Records was launched. This was a company owned and controlled by Elton and Bernie, John Reid, Steve Brown and Gus Dudgeon, and while almost certainly formed primarily to release Elton's records

Above
Elton performing live in the famous Yellow Brick Road suit which depicts the illustration featured on the front cover of the LP, 1973

Right
Elton and Bernie look delighted to receive awards of gold albums, 1973

after his commitments to DJM were completed in 1976, the idea was also for Rocket to discover and sign other acts, using the influence and expertise of the five proprietors. Announced in the music press in early 1973, it was launched in flamboyant style with a rail trip to the Cotswolds, to the picturesque English village of Moreton-in-the-Marsh in Gloucestershire, using the 'football special' train, one car of which was a discotheque. Friends, employees and the media numbered around 250 and, after they had detrained, they followed a brass band to a medieval banqueting hall where a feast was served before two of the first signings to the label, Longdancer (a group which included Kai Olsson, brother of Elton's drummer, Nigel, and Dave Stewart, later to achieve fame as Eurythmics with Annie Lennox) and singer/songwriter Mike Silver, played short showcase sets and were joined onstage by Elton and others. Davey Johnstone was another Rocket artist, releasing an album titled 'Smiling Face', on which Elton appeared and Joan Armatrading played piano, but in all honesty, Rocket would soon become first and foremost the label which released Elton's own records, although several other artists, including Kiki Dee, Judie Tzuke and folk singer Fred Wedlock, enjoyed British chart success with releases on Rocket, while both Neil Sedaka and Cliff Richard were hitmakers for Rocket in the United States.

It is worth recalling that the overwhelming majority of record labels launched by rock stars have failed to achieve lasting success –

Elton signing autographs at Paddington station on boarding the train that was to take the Rocket Records launch party to Moreton-in-the-Marsh.

Rocket*Records*

Elton with his band and John
Reid (far left), on stage at the
Rocket Records launch, 1973

Apple (the label founded by The Beatles), Rolling Stones Records, Threshold (formed by The Moody Blues), Manticore (Emerson, Lake & Palmer), T.Rex Wax Co (Marc Bolan) and 2 Tone (The Specials) all enjoyed moderate success with other acts, but ultimately the only artist-connected record label to enjoy lengthy prosperity has been Reprise, which was launched by Warner Bros to give Frank Sinatra's recordings a distinctive identity. Compared to the vast majority of such enterprises, Rocket was fairly successful until it inevitably became an unaffordable luxury for the label to attempt to support artists other than Elton himself.

This was particularly relevant after Elton began to seriously indulge his passion for football by becoming heavily involved with Watford FC, his local team when he was a boy, and whose unspectacular progress he had followed as a teenager. It was suggested that he might headline a benefit concert for Watford and that the club would welcome an investor like him; in return for purchasing shares in the club, he was given the title of vice president. This new found involvement of Elton John with football was to increase throughout the 1970s.

The immediate activity for Elton in late 1973 was his first double album, 'Goodbye Yellow Brick Road', which was not apparently planned as such; the sessions, once again at the Chateau d'Hierouville, were so productive and the results seemed so impressive that even Elton, who was initially concerned that his fans might regard a double LP as far too expensive, finally agreed that releasing it in this form was the correct thing to do. Even

then, three tracks recorded during the 'Yellow Brick Road' sessions were omitted from the album and instead used as flipsides of singles excerpted from the double LP. Those three tracks, 'Jack Rabbit', 'Whenever You're Ready (We'll Go Steady Again)' (both released with 'Saturday Night's Alright For Fighting') and 'Screw You' (the other side of the single of 'Goodbye Yellow Brick Road' itself, although it was retitled 'Young Man's Blues' for American sensibilities), did not appear on an Elton album until a 1979 DJM retrospective, and then swiftly reappeared the following year on a similar album titled 'Lady Samantha'.

Because both 'Honky Chateau' and 'Don't Shoot Me, I'm Only The Piano Player' had been recorded at the chateau, the original plan for 'Yellow Brick Road' had been to record in an even more exotic location. Elton knew that The Rolling Stones had recorded their 'Goats Head Soup' album in Jamaica, and saw no reason why he shouldn't do the same – until he got there, when it immediately became clear to him that Kingston, Jamaica, had little in common with Kingston, Surrey, other than its name, especially as the place was full of visitors there to see a world heavyweight title fight between George Foreman and Joe Frazier. Elton understandably felt somewhat insecure in this alien metropolis, and confessed that he was too scared to leave his hotel room. This turned out to be a blessing in disguise, as he spent most of his time in Jamaica with an electric piano writing the music to the lyrics which Taupin had supplied, and most of the songs on 'Goodbye Yellow Brick Road' were written there. Nor was recording in Jamaica pleasant – the studio,

Down town Kingston, Jamaica, early 1970s

which Taupin remembered was in a compound
surrounded by barbed wire guarded by
machine-gun toting security men, was less
than state-of-the-art in technical terms, and
the only track which was completed was 'a
really frantic version of "Saturday Night's
Alright For Fighting"', deemed to be unusable.
Elton then realised that the only way to
retrieve anything from this expensive fiasco
was to return to the Chateau d'Hierouville, and
the entire double album was completed in a
couple of weeks by following a regime of
working on 'three, four, five tracks a day'.

'Saturday Night's Alright' was the first
track from these sessions to be released and
it was an immediate success as a single,
peaking in the UK Top 10 and the US Top 20,
which was unusual – Elton's successes during
the early 1970s were generally bigger hits in
America than in Britain, but one reason for this
anomaly might have been that the song was
very English and reflected Bernie Taupin's
teenage years in Lincolnshire. The lyricist
apparently felt that his lyrical concentration on
America had led to neglect of his English
roots, and that this song was 'totally English'
in its conception.

Perhaps its irony prevented it from
becoming a bigger hit in America, where some
might have used it in the same way that
Charles Manson claimed he used Beatles
songs as divine instructions to wreak havoc,
and it probably received less airplay on US
Top 40 radio than usual. Many felt that its
Englishness related as much to the sound of
the track – rather Rolling Stones-ish, unsurprisingly – as to the lyrics, and it has become
a live favourite.

Elton live on stage in one of his
flamboyant costumes, 1973

Saturday Night's Alright *For Fighting*

As has the second single which came from the album, its title track: again a UK Top 10 hit, 'Goodbye Yellow Brick Road' was played almost to death on American radio to the point where it just failed to become Elton's second US Number One single of the year, although it sold a million copies to earn him a second gold single. Obviously using the very familiar imagery of the classic Judy Garland movie *The Wizard Of Oz*, the song was as much a lament as a celebration – by this time, Bernie Taupin had experienced the high life of which he had dreamed, and seemingly found it less satisfactory than he had expected. Whatever the motivation behind the lyrics, this track remains a true milestone in Elton's career, assisted in no small way by Del Newman's perfectly appropriate and completely sympathetic orchestral arrangement.

Right
Marilyn Monroe

However, neither of these hit tracks opened the album; the first track, 'Funeral For A Friend', was a striking instrumental, with engineer David Hentschel playing synthesiser and Davey Johnstone's guitar also prominent. After this lengthy piece the second part of the 11-minute plus track is 'Love Lies Bleeding', a song apparently to an ex-lover reflecting on the end of a romance. Many feel that the song which followed it, 'Candle In The Wind', a sensitive tribute to Marilyn Monroe, was even stronger. Elton later suggested that it has replaced 'Your Song' as the most popular John/Taupin composition, although surprisingly it was not one of the songs chosen to be

covered in the 'Two Rooms' tribute project. The reason for this may be that it had been a hit for Elton twice – first in the spring of 1974, when it was a major UK hit, and again in 1987/8, when it was excerpted from the 'Live In Australia' album, reaching the Top 10 on both sides of the Atlantic. Bernie Taupin later denied that he was particularly obsessed with Marilyn Monroe's sad death, suggesting that the song was less specific than that and 'could have been about James Dean'.

If 'Candle In The Wind' was a notably compassionate song, 'Bennie And The Jets', which followed it on the 'Yellow Brick Road' album, was pure fantasy – but it topped the US singles chart. A jerky rhythm accompanied the bizarre story of a presumably fictional female heavy metal star in a mohair suit with 'electric boots'. This was not released as the top side of a UK single until three years later, in 1976, when DJM Records put it out after Elton had left the label, although it was the flipside of the 'Candle In The Wind' single in 1973. In America, as 'Bennie And The Jets' was being frequently played on R&B radio, it was released instead of 'Candle' and justified the faith shown in it by becoming Elton's third million seller and his second gold single in six months. Elton later admitted that he was somewhat surprised by the chart success which greeted 'Bennie' when it was released as a single; it seemingly only came out in that format because it was being frequently programmed on R&B radio stations in Detroit, and he and Bernie Taupin, who were both fans of black music, saw this as an immense compliment: it was an even bigger buzz when it became Elton's first single to reach the *Billboard* soul-oriented Rhythm and Blues chart.

A song on the double album about which Elton and Bernie have opposing views is 'Grey Seal', which had been recorded before, at the time of the breakthrough 'Elton John' album when it was released as the B-side of the 'Rock And Roll Madonna' single. Elton was of the opinion that although he didn't understand the song's lyrics, he liked the song because the words and music together created an effect which reminded him of Procol Harum or of a painting by Savador Dali. Bernie, on the other hand, disliked his lyrics, but observed that Gary Brooker & Keith Reid, who wrote Procol's biggest hit 'A Whiter Shade Of Pale', also wrote lyrics before tunes in the same way that he and Elton worked. He called 'Grey Seal' 'oblique . . . just images'.

Another track on 'Yellow Brick Road', 'Jamaica Jerk-Off', is an affectionate reggae send-up crediting Reggae (sic) Dwight and Toots Taupin ('Toot' Hibbert was a major name in reggae during the 1970s). 'Your Sister Can't Twist (But She Can Rock & Roll)' seems quite like 'Paradise By The Dashboard Light', the track on Meat Loaf's 'Bat Out Of Hell' epic, but with Beach Boys style harmonies and an instrumental approach akin to 'Let's Dance' by Chris Montez, a star of the era when The Twist was briefly fashionable. 'Social Disease' (one of several lyrically surprising songs on the album) features Davey Johnstone on banjo. Kiki Dee, with whom Elton would duet on the chart topper 'Don't Go Breaking My Heart' in

1976, is backing vocalist on 'All The Girls Love Alice', a song about a lesbian on which percussionist Ray Cooper also guested. Oddly enough, the only song from the album included on the 1991 'Two Rooms' tribute is 'Saturday Night's Alright', which was covered by The Who.

'Goodbye Yellow Brick Road' topped the British album chart at the end of 1973 and remained in the chart for 21 months, while in the United States it topped the chart for two months and spent almost two years in the *Billboard* Top 200. As mentioned earlier in the context of 'Don't Shoot Me, I'm Only The Piano Player', this album is certified merely gold – had the platinum certification been invented in 1974, it would probably have achieved at least quadruple platinum. The double album was a major achievement in anyone's book, both artistically and of course commercially, which was somewhat less true of two further tracks which were recorded at the end of 1973, 'Step Into Christmas' and 'Ho! Ho! Ho! Who'd Be A Turkey At Christmas', which were recorded at Trident Studios in London and released as a seasonal single which reached the UK Top 30.

Elton has had several years when everything he touches turns to gold, but the 1972/3 period brought honour after honour – million selling gold singles and a first Number One, three successive gold albums which when combined topped the Billboard chart for 15 weeks of the two years, the Royal Variety Performance, Watford FC – he was certainly one of the half dozen biggest stars in the world at the end of 1973, and would remain on this plateau of popularity for some time yet.

Caribou

Whatever Gets You *Through The Night*

Don't Let The Sun

The Bitch *Is Back*

Solar Prestige *A Gammon*

Go Down On Me

You're *So Static* Pin*ky* Grims*by* Tick*ing*

Dixie *Lee*

Sick *City* The *Stinker* Cold *Highway*

Pinball *Wizard*

Lucy In The Sky

With Diamond

One Day *At A Time* Philadelphia *Freedom*

Someone Saved

Greatest *Hits*

My life Tonight

Captain *Fantastic*

Tower Of *Babel*

Days In *The Kitchen*

Better Off *Dead*

We All Fall In Love

Sometimes/Curtains

Love To Love *You Baby*

Rock Of *The Westies*

Island *Girl* Grow Some Funk *Of Your Own*

I Feel Like A Bullet *(In The Gun Of Robert Ford)*

Here And *There*

Don't Go Breaking *My Heart*

Don't Let

The Sun *Go Down*

On Me

Don't Let

The Sun Go Down On Me

Elton plays to a
capacity crowd at
Dodgers Stadium in
Los Angeles,
California, 1975

The first half of 1974 found Elton touring as
tracks from 'Goodbye Yellow Brick Road' continued to become hits. One significant event
was the arrival of John Lennon in Elton's life.
Lennon had been very supportive of Elton in
the early 1970s, so when he invited Elton to
assist him during the recording of 'Whatever
Gets You Thru The Night', a track which would
ultimately appear on Lennon's 'Walls And
Bridges' LP, Elton was delighted to assist.
This was during the period when Lennon was
separated from his second wife, Yoko Ono,
and was reportedly hell-raising in Los Angeles

'Ultimately, the decision was made to record at Caribou Ranch in the hamlet of Nederland (population under 500) in the Rocky Mountains of Colorado, but only about 30 miles from both Boulder and Denver'

with a group of drinking friends that included the singer Harry Nilsson.

The track on which Elton contributed keyboards and backing vocals seemed to be very commercial, and they agreed that if it should top the chart, as Elton expected, they would perform it together on stage.

Elton's appearance on Lennon's single was counter-balanced by the ex-Beatle appearing on one of Elton's. John Lennon socialised with Elton, Bernie and their associates for almost a year around this time, and Elton reflected that Lennon possessed a genuine humility which everyone found endearing – he even spoke of one of the best known songs by The Beatles, 'Lucy In The Sky With Diamonds', and quite seriously enquired whether Bernie Taupin recalled it!

However, before all this happened, Elton had recorded a new album, which marked his final escape from the studio in France. After the incredible success of 'Goodbye Yellow Brick Road' with its continuing array of hits, he must have wondered how he could equal such a milestone in his career, let alone top it. For the first time in three years, an album was made away from the famous 'Honky Chateau' and, in January 1974, Elton and the rest of the team (Gus Dudgeon, Davey Johnstone, Dee Murray, Nigel Olsson, Ray Cooper and, of course, Bernie Taupin and John Reid) made their first studio LP in America. Elton had already made a live album, '17-11-70' (or as Americans knew it, '11-17-70') in New York, but all eight of his previous studio albums had been recorded in Europe.

The many months of touring prevented Elton and Bernie from writing new material for an album which was contractually due to DJM, and it was felt that an exciting adventure in the country where Elton was a bona fide superstar might inspire them to write some fresh classics. Ultimately, the decision was made to record the songs at Caribou Ranch in the hamlet of Nederland (population under 500) in the Rocky Mountains of Colorado, but only about 30 miles from both Boulder and Denver. The studio was owned by James William Guercio, who was successful as a record producer, managed the popular brass/rock group Chicago, and also played bass with The Beach Boys. Elton was a long time fan of the erstwhile surfers, and several members and associates of the group were involved in the most familiar and successful track on Elton's album, 'Don't Let The Sun Go Down On Me'. Rather like the 'Honky Chateau' LP, 'Caribou' was titled after the studio where it was recorded and, also like 'Honky Chateau', it topped the US album chart (for four weeks) although, unlike that earlier LP, 'Caribou' also topped the UK album chart (for two weeks). It was a huge success in the US, remaining in the *Billboard* Top 200 albums chart for over a year, three times as long as it accumulated in Britain.

Ironically, Elton subsequently revealed that the album had to be completed in just one week due to imminent touring commitments, but even so, it not only spawned Elton's fourth million-selling single in 18 months, 'Don't Let The Sun Go Down On Me', but also included another US Top 5 single, 'The Bitch Is Back', which was supposedly inspired by a chance remark made about Elton by Bernie Taupin's American wife, Maxine.

Background
A view of the countryside outside Denver, Colorado in the region where the 'Caribou' album was recorded

Caribou

The track includes Dusty Springfield among a quartet of other backing vocalists, and the song was covered on the 1991 'Two Rooms' tribute album of cover versions of compositions written by Elton & Bernie by Tina Turner, who opened her stage show with it during the 1970s, as she thought 'the attitude of the song was right for me'.

Some time later, Elton took the stage at New York's Madison Square Garden convincingly disguised as and accurately dressed like Tina Turner . . .

Elton considered that recording 'Don't Let The Sun Go Down On Me' had been something of a milestone, as he had finally learned to patiently persevere with his vocals rather than becoming bored and frustrated after two or three abortive attempts at an ideal performance, which he attributed to being 'happier with my voice, it's plain better'. He felt that his singing had improved, and maintained that he would have been unable to sing the song well earlier in his career. He also acknowledged the influence of The Beach Boys on his work, but made it clear that he was referring to the records they made after their golden era as the spearhead of surf music, albums like 'Pet Sounds' and the ironically (and confusingly) titled 'Surf's Up', which he called 'the most perfect sounding album ever'.

'Don't Let The Sun Go Down On Me' featured a backing vocal choir of Carl Wilson and Bruce Johnston of The Beach Boys, plus Beach Boy associates Billy Hinsche and Toni Tennille. Even though it had been a massive hit (US Top 3, UK Top 20) in 1974, 'Don't Let The Sun Go Down On Me' was revived in the chart twice in 1991, first by latterday soul star

Oleta Adams, whose version appeared on the 'Two Rooms' tribute album and also became a UK Top 40 single, while at the end of that year, an even more successful version featuring Elton duetting with George Michael topped both the US and UK singles charts.

Lyrically, the least comprehensible song on the 'Caribou' album is 'Solar Prestige A Gammon'. Elton apparently instructed Bernie to write a nonsense song, as they were tired of being constantly accused of anti-semitism and indeed anti-religion in general in their songs. Even this song, however, somehow referred to five fishes, which resulted in what Elton called 'religious maniacs' making the song a cause célèbre.

'Solar Prestige' features Ray Cooper playing vibraphone – Cooper, who also appears on 'Pinky' (playing congas, watergong – whatever that may be – and vibes, as well as tambourine), 'Don't Let The Sun Go Down On Me' (bells) and 'Grimsby' (tambourine), would become Elton's right-hand man in terms of live performances a few years later.

While it is rarely regarded as among Elton's finest albums, some of the songs on 'Caribou' seem to have been generally (and unjustly) overlooked, such as 'Dixie Lily', an impressive country-flavoured song featuring soprano sax from Lenny Pickett of Tower Of Power. Various members of Tower Of Power appear on various tracks of 'Caribou', including the entire horn section of Pickett, Stephen Kupka, Emilio Castillo, Mic Gillette and Greg Adams, who blow on 'The Bitch Is Back', 'You're So Static' and 'Stinker', on which Tower Of Power's Chester Thompson also played organ.

Elton and Tina
Turner at the party for the
Tommy movie, New York, 1974

Elton on stage in *Tommy*, 1974

The final track on the album particularly grabs the attention. 'Ticking', which is somewhat cinematic, was performed by Elton without any backing musicians other than David Hentschel on synthesiser, and is not unlike a time bomb on the verge of exploding, rather like the main character of the song who suddenly killed 14 people in a bar.

Other tracks which were recorded around the same period but were omitted from the LP and instead used as B-sides to singles included 'Sick City', which appeared as the flipside of the million-selling 'Don't Let The Sun Go Down On Me'. Bernie Taupin called it "very cynical' and "another pot-shot at New York", which he actually quite liked, although as a visitor rather than as a resident, which he felt he could never become. Another song recorded at the time was 'Cold Highway', which appeared as the B-side of the single of 'The Bitch Is Back', which Taupin wrote about a friend of his from Lincolnshire who died in a car accident on a notoriously dangerous stretch of road, which they had treated as a joke until he was killed, when it suddenly became anything but amusing.

These were ultimately footnotes in Elton's career, unlike his inspired version of Pete Townshend's 'Pinball Wizard'. Elton performed the song in the Ken Russell film of the rock opera *Tommy,* in which he appeared in a cameo role. The role which Elton played so

memorably was, he maintains, originally offered to Rod Stewart, whom Elton suggests he has periodically regarded as a rival. Elton seemingly advised him against doing it, perhaps secretly hoping he may get the job for himself, as he was an obvious alternative guest celebrity for the movie. It was therefore particularly gratifying when Pete Townshend did invite him to sing the song and also appear in the film, as Townshend had been an encouraging observer during Elton's early career. The chance to work with the slightly eccentric film director Ken Russell was yet another opportunity Elton looked forward to: 'It was like doing *Top Of The Pops* with huge shoes'. Ridiculously-heeled boots and a fish-eye lens made Elton's part in *Tommy* quite unforgettable, and Rod Stewart was reportedly not amused by the turn of events.

While many, perhaps also rightly, feel that the movie was ludicrous, one of its undoubted highpoints was Elton's memorable performance, wearing massive platform boots. His version of 'Pinball Wizard' was recorded in 1974 at The Who's Ramport Studio, and when it was released as a single in Britain in 1976, it reached the Top 10.

Meanwhile, 'Whatever Gets You Thru The Night', the John Lennon track on which Elton had guested, had been released as a single and, to Lennon's great surprise, reached Number One in the US, his first solo American chart-topper. This led to several highly significant events in John Lennon's life, and indeed in Elton's. Elton had been booked to perform at Madison Square Garden in New York over Thanksgiving. The place was packed – Elton was still (and has remained) an immense live attraction – and on November 28, 1974, John Lennon kept his promise and joined Elton and his band on stage.

The two superstars performed three songs together that night: 'Whatever Gets You Thru The Night' plus a pair of Beatles classics, 'Lucy In The Sky With Diamonds' and 'I Saw Her Standing There'.

'I Saw Her Standing There' was introduced by Lennon as 'a number by an estranged fiancé', by which, of course, he meant Paul McCartney. The unexpected appearance of the ex-Beatle caused a sensation, and the evening was a riotous success, which was fortunately being recorded. It was an especially poignant occasion for John Lennon because Yoko Ono was present and visited Lennon backstage, as a result of which they were reconciled and began to live together again. About a year later, John's second son, Sean, was born, after which Lennon devoted himself to raising the child for the next five years – he had missed almost the entire childhood of his older son, Julian, because The Beatles had been at the height of their fame, and had vowed not to let the same thing happen again. In October 1980, Sean was five years old, and his father immediately recorded half a new album (the other half was by Yoko) called 'Double Fantasy'. About three weeks after the album was released, John Lennon was murdered. His brief Thanksgiving appearance with Elton John was his last-ever live show.

There was another sequel in 1974; Elton revealed that Lennon was

Elton as 'The Pinball Wizard' in *Tommy*, 1975

Right
The DM boots worn by Elton in the movie

highly flattered when other artists recorded his songs, and when he told the ex-Beatle that he was keen to cover a Beatle song, and asked Lennon for a recommendation, Lennon reckoned that no-one else had ever done 'Lucy In The Sky', and came to the studio when Elton recorded it and its B-side, 'One Day At A Time', which Elton called 'a beautiful song'.

It is true that many Beatle songs have attracted cover versions, but few, if any, artists had recorded 'Lucy In The Sky' other than Noel Harrison and Percy Faith! Elton explained: 'It's not a typical song. He came up to Caribou when we recorded it, and I did "One Day At A Time" as the B-side – I thought that was a beautiful song.' The latter was a song Lennon himself had recorded on his 1973 LP, 'Mind Games', and he contributed guitar and backing vocals to Elton's version apparently as himself – on 'Lucy In The Sky', he preferred to be credited as 'Doctor Winston O'Boogie & His Reggae Guitars'. Lennon credited himself as 'John St. John Johnston on 'Whatever Gets You Thru The Night', incidentally.

Having covered hits by The Who and The Beatles in 1974, Elton and Bernie also wrote a tribute song of their own, 'Philadelphia Freedom', for the tennis star Billie-Jean King, who was running a team of that name. Elton was still making new albums regularly, but also enjoyed recording songs

Below
Elton partners Billie Jean King in a Pro-Celebrity Tennis Tournament at Forest Hills, New Jersey, a charity event to raise funds for the Robert F. Kennedy Foundation, August 27th, 1975

specifically for release as singles, and having promised Billie-Jean that he would create a signature tune for her team, passed the baton to Bernie Taupin, who accepted the challenge, although he called it 'not exactly the easiest title to deal with'. However, this was at a time when Philadelphia briefly threatened to become the 1970s equivalent to Detroit in the 1960s, with Philadelphia International Records (with stars like The O'Jays, Harold Melvin & The Blue Notes and Billy Paul) the latterday equivalent of Motown's galaxy of stars like The Temptations, Marvin Gaye and The Four Tops. Elton was flattered that Billy Paul's biggest ever hit single, 'Me & Mrs.Jones', had a cover of 'Your Song' on its flipside, and called 'Philadelphia Freedom' 'a tribute to that music'; as a non-album single, he felt that it was the best one he had ever done, and was so pleased with it that he supplied all the backing vocals as well, a rare occurrence.

At the end of 1974, 'Lucy In The Sky With Diamonds' was released as a single which topped the US chart and reached the UK Top 10. It was Elton's third US Number One single and his second in under a year, and was the first US Number One hit of January 1975. The first US Number One of February 1975, was also associated with Elton, in that it was a Rocket Records release by Neil Sedaka. Sedaka, like Elton a piano-playing singer/songwriter, had emerged at the end of the 1950s; Elton, a great chart watcher, had noted that Sedaka's artistic renaissance in the early 1970s had occurred in the UK, where he had made an album using 10cc as his backing band, but that his rebirth had been virtually ignored in the US, where Sedaka's popularity

**Elton and John Lennon live at Madison Square Garden,
New York City, on Thanksgiving Day, November 28th 1974**

had plummeted after 1962, the year of his first Number One hit, 'Breaking Up Is Hard To Do'. He had changed record labels during this artistic rebirth but, although the UK arm of the new label had achieved success with four medium-sized hit singles, their US counterparts had managed little, if anything, in the way of chart action.

Elton intrepidly enquired whether Neil Sedaka would be interested in signing to Rocket Records for the United States and, when Sedaka enthusiastically agreed, Rocket had its first chart-topper with Sedaka's 'Laughter In The Rain'. In around two years with Rocket, Sedaka accumulated eight US hit singles, including two chart-toppers, 'Laughter In The Rain' and the 1975 million-seller 'Bad Blood' (on which Elton contributed backing vocals), a slower remake of 'Breaking Up Is Hard To Do' which made the US Top 10, as well as three major hit albums, two of which achieved gold status.

In Britain, Rocket's most immediate promise was Kiki Dee but, around the time of her arrival, a string of interesting but uncommercial acts had followed the commercially unsuccessful Longdancer and Davey Johnstone – a teenage vocalist from Wales, Maldwyn Pope, Mike Silver, who is also still around having released his 11th album in late 1994 (his third LP, 'Troubadour', was released by Rocket in 1973), and the West Country group Stackridge. None of them charted, and neither did Solution, an intriguing Dutch jazz/rock group, but Kiki Dee, whom Elton regarded as his personal project, was one artist whom the record-buying public appeared to favour.

Born Pauline Matthews, she was from Bradford in Yorkshire, where she had worked at a branch of Boots the chemist chain , before moving to London in the mid-Sixties hoping to further her vocal career which had begun as a singer with local dance bands on the ballroom circuit. In London, she met songwriter Mitch Murray, who gave her a new name and negotiated a recording contract with Philips Records. After a string of singles were notably unsuccessful, she was fortunate enough to become the first white English female singer to sign for Tamla Motown, but after a single LP with the unfortunate (in view of its commercial failure) title of 'Great Expectations', her career was in tatters. Things improved when she was invited to join Rocket in 1973, when she finally achieved her first hit single with a cover version of 'Amoureuse', a song by French-speaking singer/songwriter Veronique Sanson. English lyrics for the song were provided by Gary Osborne, who would later work much more closely with Elton. Elton took the signing of Kiki Dee very seriously indeed, producing her debut LP, 'Loving And Free' (which included 'Amoureuse'), himself with Clive Franks, the recording engineer who had worked on the 'Caribou' album, as co-producer. Not only that, he contributed two songs that he had written with Bernie Taupin, 'Lonnie And Josie' and 'Supercool', on which he and his band were the backing group, while Dee Murray played on every track on the album and Elton himself played on six titles. Although the LP didn't chart, the hit single encouraged everyone to persevere and, in 1975, Kiki Dee would enjoy further success.

Elton and Kiki Dee

Right
Elton and Neil Sedaka (right)

Elton was busy as usual, largely involved in his new post as vice president of Watford FC. He said that one of the most gratifying aspects of his work with Watford was 'mixing with ordinary people again', admitting that his lifestyle, which involved extensive touring, often made it difficult for him to appreciate how others valued normal life.

In May 1974, he had kept his promise to play a benefit concert at the Watford ground, for which he contrived to present a special guest who was also a soccer fanatic in the shape of Rod Stewart, and he also played another benefit concert around the same time, which somewhat distressed those who had expected to see him on a UK tour, which had been cancelled due to 'exhaustion'. However, Watford's fortunes remained at a low ebb in the 1974/75 season, when the team appeared to be permanently stuck in Division Four of the

Elton and Rod Stewart on stage at the Watford Football Club charity concert

Left
Elton at home in Virginia Water
in Surrey, England, 1974

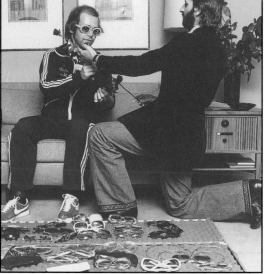

Football League. Elton tried to watch every
match that season, but it became clear that
while his personal support was welcome,
investment was what Watford needed. Before
long, Elton would provide the club with the
wherewithal required.

His second LP of 1974 was a 'Greatest
Hits' compilation which included his very first
hit, 'Border Song', plus all his biggest singles
up to and including 'Candle In The Wind',
although the latter track was omitted from the
US version of the album in favour of 'Bennie
And The Jets'. In Britain, 'Greatest Hits'
became his biggest album thus far, topping
the chart for eleven weeks of its chart life of
over 18 months, while it also reached Number
One in the US, remaining in pole position for
ten weeks of its two year residency in the
Billboard Top 200 albums.

Above
With good friend Ringo Starr. In
the foreground are some of
Elton's famous spectacles

'Captain Fantastic And The Brown Dirt Cowboy' was, according to Taupin, 'probably the finest album we've made'. It was Elton's first album to enter the *Billboard* chart at Number One

There was no reason to suppose that Elton was playing for time, as he had already completed his next LP at Caribou during the summer of 1974. This was an autobiographical collection of new songs on which Bernie's lyrics highlighted memorable events which had occurred during the formative years of the songwriting team's career. 'Captain Fantastic And The Brown Dirt Cowboy' was, according to Taupin, 'probably the finest album we've made'. It was Elton's first album to enter the *Billboard* chart at Number One, but Taupin felt that because it was a concept album, in which the songs were programmed in chronological order, it could hardly be regarded as highly commercial. The songs covered the relatively brief period from when Elton and Bernie first met to when they recorded their first LP, 'Empty Sky'. This was a time when they were establishing both personal and professional relationships, which evoked lyrics about Taupin feeling homesick and particularly Elton's quite unsuitable engagement to a female who by all accounts wore the trousers in their relationship; which ended after Elton and Bernie went out for the evening with Long John Baldry, and inspired the only hit single on the album, 'Someone Saved My Life Tonight'. Both members of the songwriting team agreed that writing the songs was an interesting and helpful experience, Taupin because he refined and rewrote his lyrics more than he ever had before, and Elton because 'it was the first album that was about me'. Elton's summing-up declared it to be 'a very, very good album musically', noting that there was no problem of running order for once because the songs had to be in chronological order.

However, the album didn't top the UK chart, although seven weeks at Number One in America was almost sufficient compensation. One rather curious aspect of the LP sleeve was that it included the lyrics of a song titled 'Days In The Kitchen', which wasn't actually on the album at all. The title track, with Davey Johnstone on mandolin and Elton playing both acoustic and electric piano, was an introduction to the characters, notable for the line 'From the end of the world to your town', while 'Tower Of Babel' includes the lines 'Sodom meet Gomorrah, Cain meet Abel'. Rather more melodic was the contagious chorus to 'Bitter Fingers', which vividly recalls the days spent writing to order. The major hit on the LP was, however, 'Someone Saved My Life Tonight', recalling the fateful evening when Bernie and Elton went out drinking with Long John Baldry, the 'sugar bear' of the song, who persuaded Elton to break off his engagement. This was a crucial song in many ways, not least because it was the album's one and only hit single and a far bigger US hit (Top 5) than it was in Britain, where it didn't quite reach the Top 20.

Of the other tracks, 'Better Off Dead' is somehow reminiscent of Queen, but another highlight is the closing medley of 'We All Fall In Love Sometimes'/'Curtains', an epic indeed, where impressive ballad melts into hypnotic repetition of 'Love To Love You Baby' with David Hentschel on synth and Elton playing both harpsichord and mellotron. 'Captain Fantastic' was released in May, 1975, and a month later, on Midsummer's Day, Elton and a virtually new band topped the bill of an open air show at London's Wembley Stadium.

Captain Fantastic

It was a glorious day and the sun shone as a succession of well-known acts played through the afternoon – Stackridge, Joe Walsh, The Eagles (before Walsh joined them, of course) and The Beach Boys. When the veteran surf music pioneers took the stage, the sun was setting, and they played about an hour's worth of their 1960s hits, which most of the audience sang with them. Elton had to follow them, as dusk and the temperature fell, and had decided to play the entire 'Captain Fantastic' album, which had only been released for a few weeks, and which many of the huge crowd had not yet heard. It was a very brave decision, and Elton was certainly appreciated, but possibly less than The Beach Boys. Perhaps it wasn't that important, as the end of Elton's time with DJM Records was in sight – one more studio album and another live one already in the can, and then independence. Rocket might sign Elton as an artist now that they had become involved with hit acts in both the United States (Neil Sedaka) and Great Britain (Kiki Dee).

By this time, Kiki Dee had had three hits in 18 months, and a second LP had been released, this time produced by Gus Dudgeon and featuring The Kiki Dee Band, a very strong quartet which included ex-Hookfoot drummer Roger Pope, young guitar prodigy Jo Partridge, and keyboard guru Bias Boshell. This second Kiki Dee album was no more successful in chart terms than its predecessor, but seemed to be an attempt to consolidate the progress made with her first Rocket album, 'Loving And Free'. On this occasion, neither Elton nor the members of his band were involved, although Gary Osborne (who

had written English lyrics to 'Amoureuse') and his songwriting partner Paul Vigrass contributed backing vocals to the final track, 'You Need Help', one of five songs written by Bias Boshell. The most successful of that five was the album's title track, 'I've Got The Music In Me', which was released as a single and became Kiki's second UK Top 20 hit.

In fact, The Kiki Dee Band was a relatively brief episode for at least one of its members because, for his Wembley spectacular, Elton had introduced a new rhythm section, as well as several other new musicians. Even though Nigel Olsson and Dee Murray had played on the 'Captain Fantastic' album, they were not invited to promote it in the live situation – Roger Pope was hired as the new drummer, and the new bass player was the diminutive American, Kenny Passarelli, whose past work had included albums with Barnstorm, the group led by Joe Walsh after he left The James Gang. Passarelli had been one of the writers (with Walsh) of 'Rocky Mountain Way', which was effectively Walsh's greatest success since he had launched his own group.

Along with Pope and Passarelli, Elton decided he needed a second guitarist in addition to Davey Johnstone, and the obvious choice, particularly because Roger Pope was now involved, was Caleb Quaye. More intriguingly, Elton also felt he needed a second keyboard player, and this vacancy was also filled by an American, James Newton Howard, whose previous achievements included work with the American singer/songwriter Melissa Manchester. With Ray Cooper and Davey Johnstone retained from the previous band, this was a major expansion and would clearly

Elton wearing a Captain
Fantastic T-shirt – the illustration
which appears on the front of
the LP and the stage backdrop
overleaf, 1975

allow Elton considerable musical variety. The
new band had started recording the next
album during the summer of 1975, making
necessary a final trip to the Caribou Ranch.
This would be released in the autumn of 1975
as 'Rock Of The Westies', the title a pun on
the familiar American phrase 'West of the
Rockies' – between the Rocky mountains and
the Pacific Ocean.

If the 'Captain Fantastic' release had
been a superior project, with its two separate
booklets included as part of the packaging,
one of memorabilia and the other of lyrics, and
a very impressive cover design featuring Elton
and Bernie in their roles as the Captain and
the Cowboy painted by the noted illustrator
Alan Aldridge, then 'Rock Of The Westies' was
relatively mundane by comparison, although
the album sleeve was luxurious, with pictures
of the participants by photographer Terry
O'Neill and the inevitable lyrics. The main
problem was that the LP lacked an obvious hit
single apart from a gentle song about a
Jamaican prostitute, 'Island Girl'.

Although it has been suggested that Elton
was extremely enthusiastic about it, in retrospect the album seems to bear the sign of
having been a contractual commitment, which
of course it was. Elton had told *Melody Maker*:
'I know that in America for the next three or
four years, I could get a gold [record] on my
name alone. As Pete Townshend said, 'I could
shit bricks and people would go out and buy
them,' and this turned out to be correct as far
as his albums were concerned, although the
sales of his singles began to decline heavily in
1977. Apart from 'Island Girl', which cannot be
faulted other than for its predictability, few of

CaptainFantastic

the songs on the album are memorable when compared with the previous treasure trove of classics. Another single was excerpted from it, coupling 'I Feel Like A Bullet (In The Gun Of Robert Ford)' – Ford shot and killed legendary outlaw Jesse James – and the Rolling Stones-like 'Grow Some Funk Of Your Own'. In the US, 'Bullet' was probably the more significant track, and in the *Billboard* chart it is registered as a double-A side. At least it made the US Top 20, unlike in the UK where 'Funk' was the favoured track, and where it completely failed to chart in early 1976.

In Britain, the album hadn't reached the Top 3, but of course it topped the US chart and went gold, with three weeks at Number One but with the briefest chart-life of any of his albums apart from the reissued 'Empty Sky', the live '11-17-70' and the 'Friends' soundtrack. The response from the record buying public was a verdict that this was not one of Elton's masterpieces – but it was the last studio album he would have to make for DJM and, from then on, he was a free agent. Nevertheless, it topped the charts, and it's hard to argue with such logic. Certainly when 'Grow Some Funk Of Your Own' failed to reach the chart, it was swiftly followed by 'Pinball Wizard' in March 1976, which wasn't released as a US single but which took Elton back into the UK Top 10 for the first time in 18 months. Also during that month of March, Elton began recording his first album for Rocket, using a studio in Canada, but with the rest of the team unchanged – Bernie, the band, Gus Dudgeon, John Reid, but by this time no Steve Brown, who had resigned from Rocket around the time of 'Caribou'.

Elton's other roles were time-consuming but apparently enjoyable. The decline of Watford had seemingly been arrested, but his investment thus far had made little difference in terms of improvement. At the end of the 1975/76 season, Elton was elected chairman of Watford. He had told *Playboy* magazine a few months earlier: 'My real ambition in life is to make enough money to retire and become chairman of my favourite soccer team, Watford FC.' When he was formally given the job, he said that he would be content if his presence drew bigger crowds to watch Watford, but explained that he was not planning to make sweeping changes immediately, and that he was not interested in 'gimmicks'.

Those who may wonder how he found himself promoted from director to chairman in two years may suspect that this rapid rise was not unconnected to the club being in debt to the tune of many thousands of pounds.

Rocket Records was a little disappointing, although its major successes of 1976, again one on either side of the Atlantic, were spectacular. Neil Sedaka had gone into artistic decline and moved to another label, but his success had sparked another idea – why not sign Cliff Richard for America, where he's virtually unknown? Britain's ultimate pop star had managed a few US hits in 1963/4, but ironically the so-called 'British Invasion' led by The Beatles probably gave him the black spot.

In 1976, Cliff released an arresting single, 'Miss You Nights', which seemed to mark an image update for the Peter Pan of Pop and which Elton thought was quite good, and a deal was struck for Cliff to be on Elton's label in the US. Cliff was automatically available to

Previous page
The stage backdrop at the open air concert held at Wembly Stadium, London. This depicts the illustration by Alan Aldridge used on the sleeve of the 'Captain Fantasic And The Brown Dirt Cowboy' LP in 1975

Elton at the Hollywood Blvd Walk Of Fame as he receieved his gold star and place in the history books as the 1,662nd entertainment lumineary to be honored on this famous sidewalk since it was completed in 1961 24th October 1975

Elton relaxes in the BBC's Paris Studios, Lower Regent Street, London, 1975.

EMI's American oulet, Capitol Records, but Capitol clearly felt that Cliff's phenomenal success in Britain was not likely to cross the Atlantic, although there were a number of Cliff fans dotted about North America. A Cliff Richard expert named the following US labels on which his singles had been released in America up to 1976: Capitol (who took his first hit, 'Move It'), ABC, Big Top, Epic (who released the 1963/4 hits), Uni (in 1968, long before Elton), Seven Arts, Monument and Sire. If Rocket wanted to have a try, what was there to lose? Elton was delighted at having the opportunity to sign another of his teenage musical heroes and, while 'Miss You Nights' didn't quite make the chart, a follow-up, 'Devil Woman', was Cliff Richard's biggest hit ever in the US, no less than 17 years after his first minor US chart entry.

After two smaller hits, Capitol took their artist back, and between 1979 and 1982 almost established Cliff as a US chart act with two more Top 10 hits, before it became clear that the only way for him to break America was to tour the country exhaustively, which his religious commitments would not leave him time to undertake. A good record would be essential to launch him in the States, and both 'Miss You Nights' and 'Devil Woman' were certainly impressive enough, but the vital aspect of Cliff's relaunch was that Elton would promote him as a legendary hero, the English Elvis, and the approval of the biggest star in the world did him no harm at all. It had been the same with Sedaka – Elton the fan wanting both to help Rocket and to restore his early pop idols to fame, which their contemporary offerings certainly deserved.

Above
Elton at the piano behind the bar
on board Staship, 1974

Right
Elton in bed on board the
Starship jet plane above
America, 1974

Bottom right (inset)
Elton poses on the tarmac with
Starship

It wasn't really so different with the much younger Kiki Dee, but she still needed that one huge hit to put her properly on the musical map. She had enjoyed a third hit in 1975 with the Kiki Dee Band, but dissent between the members of the quartet led to their break up, after which Roger Pope joined Elton. During the sessions for 'Blue Moves', Elton and Kiki recorded a truly memorable duet, 'Don't Go Breaking My Heart', which was an instant and obvious Number One. It became Elton's sixth American Number One in less than three years, but more importantly was his first ever British chart-topping single after 16 previous hits. It was also Elton's first release on Rocket Records, as he had now fully completed his contractual commitments to Dick James, who had released the live album to which DJM still had the rights in the spring of 1976.

This was 'Here And There', a fairly well-chosen album featuring, on one side, five live tracks recorded in 1974 at a benefit concert at London's Royal Festival Hall in aid of invalid children and, on the other, tracks recorded at the Thanksgiving Day Madison Square Garden show at which John Lennon had made his appearance, although the tracks on the live album do not feature the former Beatle. The Royal Festival Hall show, for which Princess Margaret was in the audience, took the form of a brief musical history of Elton's career. 'Skyline Pigeon' was performed solo, then Dee Murray and Nigel Olsson came on for 'Border Song', Davey Johnstone and Ray Cooper arrived for 'Honky Cat', with good solos from Johnstone on lead guitar and Cooper on duck call (an instrument like a kazoo), before a final chorus of 'Oh! Susannah'. Lesley Duncan then

sings 'Love Song' as a duet with Elton, a rare treat, before a closing rave-up with 'Crocodile Rock'. The American side also has its moments – an impressive opening 'Funeral For A Friend'/'Love Lies Bleeding' followed by 'Rocket Man', which is greeted with a scream from the audience. 'Bennie And The Jets' seems no more interesting than usual, and 'Take Me To The Pilot' which was undoubtedly memorable for those watching it when it was performed,is less listener-friendly without the benefits of the audience atmosphere and the spectacle of the stage show.

Considering what it was, 'Here And There' didn't do at all badly – it made the US Top 5, was five months in the chart and went on to be certified gold, and was the twelfth gold album released by Elton in six years; it reached the Top 10 in Britain and was listed for two months – but meanwhile preparations were being made for the first Rocket album, which all concerned were determined was going to be special. Elton expended a lot of time and trouble on the album, which was planned to be a double LP, while also announcing that he would be giving up live work to concentrate on his duties as chairman of Watford Football Club.

Unfortunately, and to many, surprisingly, the Number One hit didn't do a great deal for Kiki Dee's career. A reissue which coupled her first hit, 'Amoureuse', with the title track of the 'Loving And Free' album (which Elton had produced), almost reached the Top 10 in the autumn of 1976, but the duet with Elton was a tough act to follow. In 1977, Elton and Clive Franks produced another album for Kiki, which was titled simply 'Kiki Dee'.

Right
Greeting the 70,000 strong crowd at the famous Dodger Stadium, Los Angeles, California, summer 1975

Dodgers *Stadium*

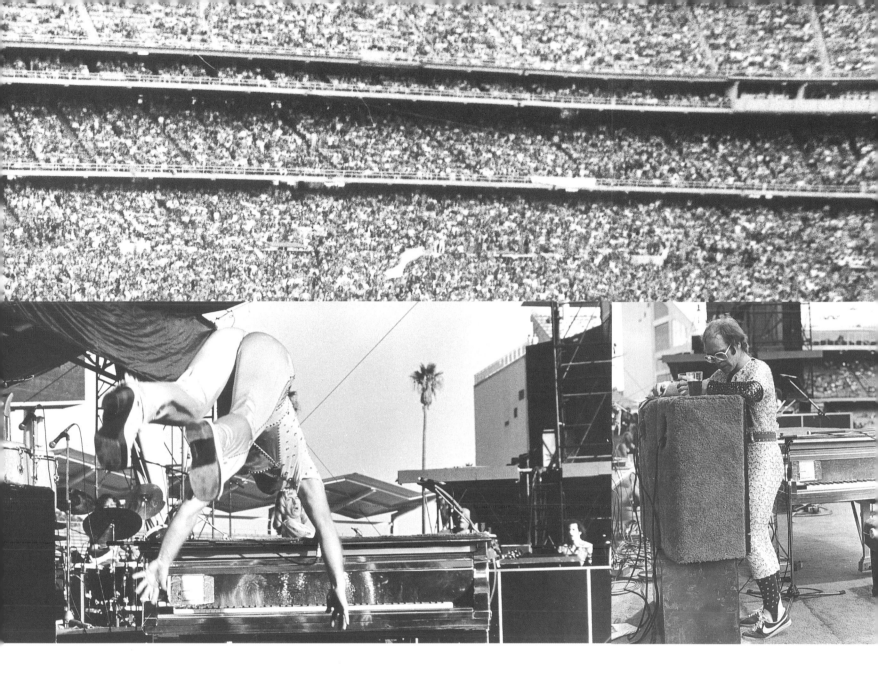

Elton's two concerts at the famed Dodgers Stadium in Los Angeles were a sell-out within ninety minutes of the tickets going on sale, with a total of a hundred and twenty thousand people filling the home of the city's baseball team for an incredible three and a half hour show. The previous time a rock act had featured at the stadium was back in 1966 when it played host to The Beatles, and there were inevitable comparisons made with this superstar of the Seventies and his predecessors from the Sixties. As Elton performed his vocal and physical acrobatics in one of the greatest performances of his career, there in his line-up of backing vocalists (left) was the 1975 Wimbledon champion, tennis star Billie Jean King.

Far left
Elton with Cher, 1975

Left
Bernie Taupin

An all-star cast of musicians included Davey Johnstone, James Newton Howard, Ray Cooper, Bias Boshell, Dee Murray, Steve Holley, who went on to drum with Paul McCartney's Wings, and a collection of American brass players, Electric Light Orchestra members and well-known backing singers. The album charted for a few weeks but peaked outside the UK Top 20. It did include a couple of medium-sized hit singles in Boshell's 'First Thing In The Morning' and an American song, 'Chicago', on which noted arranger and conductor Gene Page directed the orchestra, but the album as a whole could hardly be seen as a step forward. The other bizarre aspect of the Kiki Dee affair was that the composers of the million-selling duet were credited as 'Ann Orson/Carte Blanche', names which had actually already been used on 'Hard Luck Story', a track on 'Rock Of The Westies' on which Kiki had been one of the backing vocalists. The joke was that the name of the composers was horse and cart . . .

Victim

Victim *Of* Love

With the DJM years now behind him, Elton began a new phase of his career with the 'Blue Moves' double LP, which was released during the autumn of 1976, and quickly rose to the Top 3 of the American album chart, which wasn't at all a disaster, although his previous six new studio LPs, from 'Honky Chateau' to 'Rock Of The Westies', had all reached the Number One spot and had been certified gold. Strangely, 'Blue Moves' was the first Elton John album to be certified platinum, as 1976 was the year when the platinum awards were introduced.

The double album was a very ambitious project, and included 18 tracks, of which some were instrumentals, like the brief (under 90 seconds) opener 'Your Starter For Ten' (titled after the phrase used in the TV quiz University Challenge). The tune, which was written by Caleb Quaye (once again sharing

BlueMoves

Edith Piaf, the tragic French *chanteuse*: "Cage The Songbird" (from 'Blue Moves') was a tribute to her

guitar duties with Davey Johnstone) had little, if anything, to do with the TV show, and the same was true of the similarly brief 'Theme From A Non-Existent TV Series', credited to both Elton and Bernie as writers, despite its lack of lyrics. The third instrumental, 'Out Of The Blue', was much weightier and was regarded in some circles as overlong – when the album was initially released as a compact disc in the early 1980s, the decision was made to omit three tracks from the double album in order that 'Blue Moves' could be released as a single CD, and 'Out Of The Blue' was one of those which was not selected.

Two other tracks were similarly missing from the original double album when it was digitalised: 'Shoulder Holster', which was more or less a rewrite of the familiar 'Frankie & Johnny' story, featured a horn section that included The Brecker Brothers (who were a hit act on their own account, as well as world class session players) and the celebrated sax player David Sanborn, while 'The Wide-Eyed And Laughing' boasted backing vocals by David Crosby and Graham Nash, who were obviously in a period when they were not working with their supergroup partners,

Stephen Stills and Neil Young. Considering the ex-Byrd and the erstwhile Hollie were involved, it seems odd that the track was omitted from the CD, although their part in 'Cage The Songbird', an impressive tribute to the great French singer Edith Piaf, was an essential inclusion on the CD.

Literally scores of singers and players appeared on the album – one good example was 'Tonight', a heavily-orchestrated ballad which in places brought Jimmy Webb's 'MacArthur Park' to mind, and showcased Elton backed by the London Symphony Orchestra, whose contribution was arranged and conducted by James Newton Howard, and recorded at Abbey Road studios in London. Another was 'One Horse Town', which was more of a rocker, featuring The Martyn Ford Orchestra which was arranged and conducted by Paul Buckmaster and again recorded at Abbey Road – and they were at the beginning of the album.

In much the same way that almost any double album is regarded by critics as over-long, there was a feeling that while 'Blue Moves' was interesting and by no means a disaster, it would have been a much stronger

Sorry Seems To Be

The Hardest Word

single LP. The only major hit single it spawned was 'Sorry Seems To Be The Hardest Word', which sold a million in the US during a three months plus spell in the *Billboard* Hot 100, and almost reached the UK Top 10, although unwary British record buyers may have been distracted because DJM had released 'Bennie And The Jets' only a month before 'Sorry' emerged; the DJM track was only a modest hit, just creeping into the UK Top 40, but it may have caused enough confusion to hinder the brand new track's chances of Top 10 success. This again boasted strings, conducted and arranged by James Newton Howard, who also wrote the arrangement for an accordion, while Ray Cooper played vibraphone, although the track otherwise lacked a drummer. Bernie Taupin recalled that because the previous two albums, 'Captain Fantastic' and 'Rock Of The Westies', had both entered the US chart at Number One, there was a general feeling of pressure surrounding the team, who wondered whether it was possible to achieve the feat three times in a row.

Although there was a gap of a year between the two albums, they were recorded only nine months apart, and the need for 'Blue Moves' to be something extra special, as Elton's debut offering on his own label, was obviously considerable. Elton later reflected that it was their intention to make every album very different from its predecessor, but what resulted with 'Blue Moves' was, he felt, 'blatantly uncommercial'. He also mentioned the artistic pressure which surrounded the project, called it 'very poignant'; he went on to describe some of the lyrics as 'real desperate', but concluded 'I just love the album'.

Victim Of Love

Bernie Taupin's lyrics here are rarely, if ever, upbeat, unless you count the interminable 'Bite Your Lip (Get Up And Dance)', with Davey Johnstone on slide guitar and a gospel choir directed by the Rev. James Cleveland: Cleveland and his funky combo had appeared on an Aretha Franklin album, as well as one by The Blues Brothers. This track was far from subtle and those who expected more from an Elton John track than six and a half minutes of undeniably funky dance music with little in the way of lyrical meat felt rather choked when it was released as the third single from the album in the summer of 1977 – it really wasn't a second 'Oh Happy Day', and perhaps wasn't even designed as such.

Even the hit was lyrically defensive, and it transpired that Taupin was feeling dejected when he was writing the lyrics for the songs, principally because his marriage to his 'blue-jean baby, L.A. lady' had encountered stormy weather. His Maxine, who had been happy to live in a mansion in Lincolnshire when they were first an item, was probably bored, while Bernie himself led the life of a rock star without the responsibility of going onstage, other than for the encores. He reasonably enough expected Maxine to be his globe-trotting female Passepartout, but it wasn't that easy, because Elton's band were all male, and according to Philip Norman's Elton biography, she finally vented her frustration by having an affair with Kenny Passarelli, a fellow American.

In 'Between Seventeen And Twenty', Taupin bemoaned his fate, recalling happier days when they had fallen in love, with five backing vocalists providing an authentic Beach Boys vocal sound. (Which wasn't too

hard as the quintet included a member of that group, Bruce Johnston, as well as his protégé, Curt Becher, who had produced the breakthrough album by The Association, another group who used multiple vocals in an original manner.) As an incidental, Becher was known as Curt Boettcher in the 1960s, but was advised to simplify the spelling of his surname by some voodoo merchant. Becher died before he was 50 . . .

Arguably the most intricate vocal arrangement came on 'Chameleon', where seven backing singers, including Johnston, Becher and Toni Tennille, embellish Bernie's resigned lament on his ex-love, but no such vocal smoothness softened the desperate 'If There's A God In Heaven (What's He Waiting For?)'. The second single from the album was 'Crazy Water', five and a half minutes of not very much which wasn't released as a US single and just crept into the UK Top 30 in the spring of 1977. In America, they had gone straight for 'Bite Your Lip', which with 'Chameleon' as its B-side might pick up useful sales. It limped into the US Top 30, and when it was released in Britain it did the same.

Record buyers may recall that the summer of 1977 was the time of Queen Elizabeth II's Silver Jubilee, and the act grabbing all the headlines was a quartet called The Sex Pistols. 1977 was the year when ABBA were on tour, The Bee Gees were filling discotheques with their 'Saturday Night Fever' hits, and Elton seemed like old news. 'Sorry Seems To Be The Hardest Word' was fine, but neither 'Crazy Water' nor 'Bite Your Lip' had a hope. Although Elton had no big hits, there was a single in which he was involved released at

Elton, in 1978 with the football commentator Jimmy Hill (left) and comedian Eric Morecambe at a charity auction in aid of The Goaldiggers sporting charity, to raise money for playing areas for underpriviledged children throughout Britain.

this time which has become highly collectable, although maybe more for its scarcity than its aesthetic qualities. Titled 'Jimmy, Brian, Elton, Eric', only 500 copies were pressed of this item which featured soccer journalists/ TV pundits Jimmy Hill and Brian Moore, plus Elton and comedian Eric Morecambe, who was a big fan of Luton Town FC. The (very) limited edition was sold (or more likely auctioned) for the benefit of a charity, for under-previlidged children, called The Goaldiggers.

The rise of punk/rock was not something which Elton could appreciate, as its musical values were diametrically opposed to those of

a student of The Royal Academy Of Music. Most of the punks seemed to chiefly rely on youth and enthusiasm, with musical skill very low on their priority list. Neither could he identify with their confrontational attitude, or their supposedly revolutionary fashions of mutilation – why would anyone enjoy sticking a nappy pin through their cheeks and safety pins in their ears, lips and nostrils? It was at this point that rather a lot changed for Elton, in many aspects of his life. He decided to retire from touring (although it was made clear in an interview with Cliff Jahr which appeared in *Rolling Stone* magazine that there was little

likelihood of a permanent absence from the stage). He maintained that his instincts (to which he always paid attention) told him to slow down - as he pointedly enquired, 'Who wants to be a 45 year old entertainer in Las Vegas like Elvis?'

He also seemed to realise that he was at an important point in his career: He felt that he was at a second milestone with the new album, which he hoped would be a continuation of his upward progress in terms of success and popularity, but which included, he revealed, 'some surprises' in the shape of

some downbeat love songs with 'jazzy type tinges', and likened it to his eponymous breakthrough album.

It also came out that Elton had written part of the lyric to 'Don't Go Breaking My Heart', and he said: 'I'd like to branch out into words.' In retrospect, this could have been an early coded message about an impending separation between The Captain and the Cowboy, as would become clear in 1978.

An end to touring also meant an end to paying retainers to the band, and perhaps more importantly allowed plenty of spare time

Left
Elton at home in Windsor in his
office, 1976

Elton and the Watford football
team, 1979

in which Elton could plan Watford FC's rise to a higher plateau. He decided that what was needed was a new manager for the club, and set his sights very high. The brightest young managerial star of the era was Graham Taylor, who had worked wonders with the unfashionable Lincoln City FC, and Elton pursued him. Taylor could see little point in leaving the team he had inspired to relative prominence to live in London and attempt to revive a club whose chairman was a pop star, but Elton was persistant, and after Taylor took over Watford rapidly improved, gaining promotion from Division Four to Division Three in his first season. Elton declared: 'The feeling of promotion was better than having a record at Number One.' Asked what his immediate ambition was for Watford, he replied: 'Third Division champions and promotion again. There's no point in consolidating, you've got to be positive in football.' At the end of the next season, Watford were not Third Division champions but they were promoted to the Second Division and reached the semi-final of a cup competition; to celebrate the event, Elton used the Watford team as backing vocalists on a couple of tracks of his next album.

However, the major revelation of the *Rolling Stone* interview was that Elton was bisexual. It had hardly been a secret that Elton was regarded by gossip columnists as a 'confirmed bachelor', but he had never admitted as much before. However, he was adamant that he and Bernie Taupin had never been lovers despite the fact that everyone assumed they had been, and that their relationship was essentially fraternal, which he supposed was why they had remained partners. This certainly

rings true, as the duo seem to have remained on friendly terms even when their partnership was on ice at the end of the 1970s. Elton also denied that there had ever been a 'serious person' during his life. He also remarked that Taupin's 'whole situation is up in the air'.

Looking back, it can be seen that there was an imminent split – perhaps Taupin's morose outlook had persuaded Elton that if he continued to record songs like 'If There's A God', his already decelerating career might come to a full stop, so it might be better for them to pursue their own interests separately for a while. Elton had found in Watford the kind of challenge to keep him busy, and Bernie was hanging out in Los Angeles with Ringo Starr and other members of rock's aristocracy, trying to come to terms with his wife's infidelity.

Given time, Bernie would hopefully get over his traumas, and meanwhile, there were a few recording projects that Elton had been considering. He needed to change his musical approach to perhaps win grudging respect from the likes of messrs. Rotten, Vicious, Strummer and co., and a fresh musical direction was one way to go about it. The band had gone, Bernie had gone, touring too was suspended, and Rocket was in transition because its head of A&R, Gus Dudgeon, had decided to resign. Dudgeon always seemed somewhat remote from the rest of Elton's inner circle, although he was obviously very close professionally; he had retained his independence by working with some success with other artists, especially Lindisfarne, the Newcastle folk/rock quintet, whose triumphant comeback LP, 'Back And Fourth', included a Top 10 single.

There was interest being expressed by other artists, and according to Philip Norman's *Definitive Biography*, Dudgeon wasless than happy with the way Rocket was heading, and had supposedly been miffed when told that Dave Edmunds, who he was keen to sign to Rocket, was past it. Literally a few days later, the Welsh guitar star was signed to Led Zeppelin's Swansong label, for which he made seven hits in four years. Dudgeon was also unhappy with the way the company was run, with its directors scattered to various parts of the world, which meant that making decisions was too time-consuming. As already mentioned, he had maintained his independence and was a valued part of the success story, but after tasting such fame, was unsure of Elton's future direction and after so many gold albums in succession, felt he needed a fresh challenge. Under such circumstances, it would not be feasible for Gus Dudgeon to continue producing Elton . . .

Dudgeon's replacement as Rocket's A&R boss even signed a punkish 'mod' band known as The Lambrettas to the label in 1980. Their debut Top 10 hit was a cover of the Fifties R&B classic 'Poison Ivy', and a follow-up made the Top 20, but then came what seemed to be an ultimately contrived single – released under the title 'Page Three', it was a fairly crass song about the Sun newspaper. The Sun supposedly took out an injunction to suppress the single on the ludicrous grounds that use of the words 'Page Three' was some kind of copyright infringement and mightin some way damage the tabloid's credibility. After this publicity, The Lambrettas reissued the record using a different title, and it was in and out of the chart in a month, after which the group seemingly faded away.

Rocket didn't have much to cheer about beside Elton, and he was going through changes. In the autumn of 1977, he recorded with a black American producer named Thom Bell, who had been one of the architects of the 'Philly sound' which Elton found so very enjoyable. It is interesting that nothing from these sessions was released until 18 months after they were recorded, due to unfortunate personality clashes between the artist and producer. The move was apparently prompted by Elton's admiration for records by Philly soul acts like The Spinners and The Stylistics, which he called 'very dry sounding', and he confessed that Bell had commented somewhat negatively on his singing, claiming that it was written in too high a key for comfort. This, Elton later found was quite correct, although he said 'I wasn't very pleased with him telling me at the time'.

When Bell told Elton he didn't breathe properly, the die was cast. Only three tracks from these sessions were released, none of which involved Elton as a songwriter, and although he probably fulfilled an ambition by recording with members of MFSB (which is an acronym of 'Mother, Father, Sister, Brother') and The Spinners, the results were unspectacular because the songs were only average. It becomes clear why nothing was released for so long, and even then only after Elton and Clive Franks had remixed the tracks. This duo also produced the next single by Elton which was released, 'Ego', a song for which Bernie Taupin had apparently written the lyrics some time before.

Elton with his double – a wax model of himself commissioned by the famous Madame Tussauds waxwork museum, London. At a cost of £1,000 the lookalike delivers a speech welcoming visitors to the exhibition. This made him the first talking pop star at the exhibition, 1976

'Ego' was released in the spring of 1978, but by Elton's high standards was a commercial failure. He was already working on his next album, which would be the first one without input from Bernie Taupin. There was no great rush to release anything immediately, as the summer was well-known to be the time when fewer records were sold, and there may have been a hint that DJM were planning a major back catalogue campaign for the autumn: a special release of a dozen singles in a box, plus a 12" (for better sound quality) of 'Funeral For A Friend' and 'Love Lies Bleeding' (from 'Yellow Brick Road'), and 'We All Fall In Love Sometimes' and 'Curtains' from 'Captain Fantastic'. A very strong release, and although it didn't make the chart, it certainly kept Elton on the radio while he was recording a new LP. A fortnight after all the reissues, the first fruits of the new recording sessions were released in the shape of a single, 'Part Time Love', which was a Top 20 hit in Britain, and almost the same in America.

It was a hit, even if not a major work, but for the new songwriting team of Elton and Gary Osborne, a promising start. Osborne had written the English lyrics to 'Amoureuse', and was well-liked and good company, but as a lyricist, was a good craftsman rather than an inspired artist, who was best known as a writer of advertising jingles rather than major songs. Where the previous songwriting credits had been widely understood to mean that Bernie Taupin wrote the words, which Elton then set to music, the division had now become less clearcut, and there was a suspicion that far from the minor changes Elton had made to Bernie's songs (usually for musical

reasons), with Osborne, Elton, as the senior partner, had taken a far greater lyrical role.

Another reason why Elton seemed to be far more involved than usual was Watford Football Club, and another curious aspect of 'A Single Man', the LP on which 'Part Time Love' was included, was that on two of the tracks, 'Big Dipper' and 'Georgia', the backing vocal choir included the Watford team. In *The Elton John Tapes*, a book published in 1981 featuring a lengthy interview between Elton and BBC Radio One disc jockey Andy Peebles, Elton noted that 'A Single Man' was not originally planned as an album. His first spell in the studio had produced 'Ego', whose lyrics (by Taupin) had been written two years before, and a new song written by Elton with Gary Osborne, 'Shine On Through'. Elton admitted that because he had written precious little in the recent past, he was desperate to get back in the swing, and incautiously had attempted to change the habits of a lifetime by writing melodies first, rather than fitting a melody to virtually completed lyrics; however, he reckoned 'we had great fun'.

Elton later denied that there was any intention of a permanent end to his partnership with Bernie Taupin, conceding, however, that they both needed to work with different collaborators. His own 'A Single Man' (a title with several shades of meaning) had been achieved with Gary Osborne's assistance, while Taupin had completed an album with Alice Cooper 'so people put two and two together'. He also mentioned that he and Bernie were living on opposite sides of the Atlantic, which clearly made working together difficult, and expressed the opinion that both

Elton photographed with Wings members Paul and Linda McCartney at the Capital Radio Music Awards, London, March 1978. Elton's award was for the best concert of 1977.

Left
Elton receiving the Capital Radio Music Award, 1978

Song For Guy

had been afflicted by jealousy, but realised that a break would be appropriate.

Another scenario might have been that Elton soon realised that he wasn't a born lyricist, and used Osborne as both a thesaurus and sometimes as a plot source. Certainly the magical chemistry of the longstanding partnership with Taupin was absent, but Elton was somewhat reassured that his talent had not evaporated when the new album, 'A Single Man', spawned what was undoubtedly a classic single, 'Song For Guy', which went Top 5 in Britain, although it was completely overlooked in America. This was, unfortunately for the new writing team, an instrumental written solely by Elton, and there was a story behind it. Guy Burchell was a motorcycle messenger who worked at Rocket and was killed in an accident at the age of 17.

He mentioned classical composers Elgar and Handel as people whose work made him tearful, and 'music that would be played at funerals, church music' and confessed himself fascinated with music involving death, such as 'Funeral For A Friend' and 'Song For Guy' among his own compositions.

According to *The Elton John Tapes*, 'Song For Guy' was written, recorded and finished on the same day, although that seemingly wasn't its original title, and it was only called 'Song For Guy' when Elton heard of Guy Burchett's tragic death and realised how appropriate the tune was to commemorate that event.

In the US they clearly had no idea how good it was, and when it stiffed, Elton had an interesting follow-up – he and Clive Franks had remixed the three tracks from the Thom

Bell sessions, and they were hopefully now suitable for release. All three songs had been written by Leroy Bell and Casey James, a duo who made their own hit album in 1978, which was produced by Thom Bell, Leroy Bell's uncle. The remix meant little in Britain where 'Are You Ready For Love' was the song which was promoted, and the single failed to reach the Top 40, but in the US, 'Mama Can't Buy You Love' was a Top 10 hit, Elton's first for two and a half years. In the US, the entire three songs were released as a so-called 'mini-album' titled 'The Thom Bell Sessions', which thus qualified for the *Billboard* Top 200 Albums chart, where it was listed for over four months, peaking just outside the Top 50.

Next came an even more unexpected innovation. As well as his interest in the Philly sound (as exemplified by Thom Bell), Elton was also intrigued by the European dance music of the time, much of which emerged from Munich in Germany, where producers Giorgio Moroder and Pete Bellotte were enjoying major success with Donna Summer. It transpired that Elton and Bellotte were old friends, as both had played together at the Top Ten Club in Hamburg, Elton with Bluesology and Bellotte with the support band, although they had subsequently lost contact until Elton had realised from a Donna Summer album that his old mate was making big international hits. Bellotte contrived to meet Elton in London, and asked whether there was any chance of them making an album together, to which Elton agreed, as long as he didn't need to write any of the material or to play on the record. A short half day trip to Germany from Switzerland (where he was writing the songs for his next full-length LP, '21 At 33') was all the time it took him. Admitting that it was probably not a smart career move, Elton defiantly added: 'I don't regret doing it', stating that his aim was to make a record to which discriminating night club patrons could dance, but dubbing it 'self-indulgent'. FM radio in America, which had generally been strongly supportive of Elton's work kept the album well away from their turntables, only relenting when they found there were some notable US players involved.

Elton and Wreckless Eric (with towel) and other Stiff Records artists at Watford Town Hall, 1978, during a Stiff Records tour

Having decided to use Bellotte as producer of his next LP, and perhaps because he was very busy with his Watford duties, allowing Bellotte to prepare the original songs and provide the musicians perhaps in retrospect may have not been the smartest musical decision Elton ever made. Apart from the opening track, an eight minute plus version of the Chuck Berry classic, 'Johnny B.Goode', in the approximate style of Dave Edmunds and sounding very authentic, the album, which

was titled 'Victim Of Love', was for some little more than an unrelenting sequence of over 25 minutes of music with repetitive lyrics and few redeeming qualities with no breaks.

The songs (apart from 'Johnny B. Goode' – and who would expect that a cover of a 20-year-old Chuck Berry song would be the obvious highlight of an Elton John album in 1979?) were written by Bellotte and various collaborators, and after the basic tracks were laid down in Munich, the recordings were taken to Los Angeles for overdubs. Among the American musicians who lent a hand were Tower Of Power sax player Lenny Pickett, who blows up a storm on 'Johnny B.Goode', Steve Lukather of Toto (a group who were one of Elton's favourites of that era, by all accounts), who added guitar solos to both 'Born Bad', a track which seemed to be in the style of Chic, a very popular dance act of the late Seventies, and the workmanlike Eurodisco of 'Warm Love In A Cold Climate', while Patrick Simmons and Mike (sic) McDonald of The Doobie Brothers added backing vocals to the album's hypnotic title track, which was released as a single and became a minor US hit, although it generated little attention in Britain. McDonald later began to use his full first name, and as Michael McDonald became a solo star in the first half of the 1980s.

The comparative failure of both these dance-oriented projects, on top of the cool response to 'A Single Man', was a fairly minor item compared to a genuinely pioneering undertaking in which Elton was the key player. In the spring of 1979, he had returned to live performance after an absence of over a year. The idea was not to reassemble a full band,

A poster advertising Elton's tour of Russia in 1979

but to work as a duo with percussionist Ray Cooper. Cooper is one of the great showmen of rock music, who can effortlessly capture the attention of any audience with his charismatic and very theatrical approach to the banging of a tambourine or scraping a guirro. Elton no doubt felt that Cooper was a visual perfect foil for his stage work performances, not only as a stunning percussion player but also as a focal point for audiences who required something more to watch than a singing keyboard player, even if the pianist in question was at the time nothing less than the most popular live rock performer in the world.

Elton on stage during one of his concerts in Russia, August 1979

Left
Performing onstage with Ray Cooper, 1979

The return to performance became a tour of several countries on the European side of the Atlantic, and according to Philip Norman's Elton biography, it was Elton's own idea to tour in Russia, where few Western rock stars had ever ventured – one who had was Cliff Richard, whose standing at that time in the rock star pantheon was considerably below that of Elton. This was some time before the

glasnost and perestroika reforms introduced by Mr.Gorbachev, although there was little doubt that there was considerable interest in Western popular music in the USSR. Perhaps the feeling that he was unlikely to be judged in the context of the newly-fashionable punk bands, The Sex Pistols and the rest, who would hardly be known in the USSR, was one of the reasons for Elton's decision to take this unique opportunity to make history.

The tour, which was organised by Harvey Goldsmith, the most influential promoter in Europe (and possibly the entire world), took place in May 1979, and it was arranged that one of the concerts would be broadcast live on BBC Radio One, while a documentary film was made of the trip. It included concerts in both Moscow and Leningrad, and was inevitably an immense success, although to Elton the Russian visit was also a chance to review his repertoire and discover whether the old songs he and Bernie had written were as impressive as others claimed they were, something about which he was not certain himself. Elton took the unique opportunity offered of creating a completely new live repertoire, and revealed that the discipline of working with just his piano and a percussionist had made him consider the meaning of the lyrics very carefully, and had also resulted in an improvement in his vocal delivery. He had 'rediscovered the songs', and realised that because of his constant (and admirable) desire to progress, he had overlooked and often undervalued them, and had refused to take seriously compliments paid to them, but he was pleased to confirm that he had been wrong. Having to re-learn a number of songs

Elton bewigged lampoons his
longtime friend Rod Stewart

Above
Elton and his band in China,
1977

Opposite
In concert, 1977

which he had excluded from his stage show
for some time forced him to concentrate; and
concentration was another discipline he had
recently overlooked.

Elton was delighted with the historic
Russian trip, which he correctly regarded as a
major achievement, although he claimed that
the original idea of the tour with Ray Cooper
was to convince himself that he wanted to
start playing concerts again after what had
been for him an eternity away from the foot-
lights. Initially, it was to have been nothing
more than a few European dates, but the challenge of performing the first half of the show
totally solo, and then inviting Cooper to join
him for the second half was one which he
eagerly accepted, and which he intemperately
enjoyed, as he could follow his own instincts,
interspersing ballads and rock as he felt
appropriate. He warmed to the people and
events he experienced in Russia, and cried as
he travelled from Leningrad to Moscow and
left behind hundreds of fans who had followed
him everywhere.

By the end of a decade which had seen
him achieve superstardom and, more to the
point, retain it for five years while any other
contenders watched his progress with envy,
after which he (and innumerable others) were
reviled by a younger generation of punk rockers who regarded the kind of lifestyle enjoyed
by Elton and his peers as reprehensible
(although that was probably not the word they
used). Elton began a decline in his record success after the one-off duet with Kiki Dee, and
for many of his admirers, only seemed to
recapture the magic in 1982, by which time
most of the punks had disappeared.

Victim Of Love

However, this was the period when he was most involved with Watford FC. Among many worthy Watford players of that era, two particularly stand out from the rest, John Barnes and Luther Blissett. Both played for England and both were black – Blissett scored more goals for Watford than anyone else has ever achieved, but his international career was brief compared with that of Barnes, who is still

in contention as an England player. However, Watford struggled in their first season in Division Two, but as they had been in the Fourth Division only a year before, it was far from surprising; in the 1980/81 season, they finished in the top half of the table, and Elton could justifiably be proud of what the club had achieved under his chairmanship.

What was clearly needed at the start of the new decade was a big album. The last big success had been with 'Blue Moves' in 1976, and that, of course, had been with Bernie Taupin's lyrics. It would obviously be a good idea for Bernie to be represented on a new album, even if he wasn't the only lyricist involved. Then someone evolved a clever concept – in 1980, Elton would be 33 years old, and by that age, he would have released 21 albums, thus '21 At 33' it was, and to have recorded so much at such a speed was actually a considerable achievement, although the number of albums includes compilations and even the mini-album. Not that it could matter to any but the most mean-spirited . . .

Still with Clive Franks as engineer and co-producer, the nine tracks on '21 At 33' featured lyrics by no less than four collaborators: Bernie Taupin and Gary Osborne wrote three each, Tom Robinson two and Judie Tzuke the closing 'Give Me The Love'. Tzuke was arguably Rocket's most interesting discovery of the years when the label was winding down to the point where Elton was its only artist. An attractive blonde, Tzuke was also a better than average aspiring songwriter, and in 1979, had reached the UK Top 20 with a highly original single released by Rocket and titled 'Stay With Me Till Dawn', but her collaboration with Elton was not continued.

The union with Tom Robinson, who enjoyed success on the strength of his biggest hit '2-4-6-8 Motorway', but perhaps someone motivated by more than nihilism and anarchy if his anthemic 'Glad To Be Gay' was anything to go by, was intriguing. The gay pride song was something with which Elton could empathise.

He had mentioned in the revealing 1976 piece in Rolling Stone that he was still looking for a soul-mate 'of either sex' and suspicions were confirmed, thus working with Tom Robinson wasn't such an unlikely idea. One of the songs Elton and Robinson wrote, 'Never Gonna Fall In Love Again' was pleasantly melodic but its chances of pop radio play were lessened by lines like 'Lechery can be such fun'. The other song co-written with Robinson, 'Sartorial Eloquence', was a single and a minor hit on both sides of the Atlantic as the follow-up to the biggest chart success on the album, 'Little Jeanie', a Gary Osborne-assisted pop song with a melodic chorus, which reached the US Top 3 and the UK Top 40. Osborne's other two songs also had their moments, especially 'Dear God', on which the backing singers included Toni Tennille, Bruce Johnston, Peter Noone (Herman of Herman and The Hermits fame) old uncle Curt Becher and all. Very classy harmonies.

The three songs with words by Bernie Taupin were not singles material, although one of them, 'Two Rooms At The End Of The World', has emerged as a special item in the John/Taupin songbook, not least because it was the title of the 1991 all-star tribute album which celebrated the compositions of Elton & Bernie. In the companion book, also titled *Two Rooms*, Bernie Taupin felt that 'Two Rooms At The End Of The World' was the song which summed up his relationship with Elton. Somewhat ironically, the song in question, 'Two Rooms', was not one of the songs that was covered on the tribute album.

In *The Elton John Tapes*, Elton explained that he and Bernie Taupin had remained in

contact when they were not writing songs together. He had not only used other collaborators, such as Judie Tzuke, Tom Robinson and Gary Osborne, and claimed that he had actively encouraged Taupin to experiment with other songwriters. At that time, Taupin was working with Rod Stewart (of all people) on songs for a projected Taupin solo album, and, in Elton's words, 'there was never any feud'; Taupin's lyrics to the track 'Two Rooms At The End Of The World' (from the '21 At 33' album) explained it all. Another track from the album, 'White Lady White Powder', involved very famous backing vocalists, as the vocal harmonies Elton envisaged on the song could only be performed by country/rock superstars The Eagles, who were old friends, of course. Three members of The Eagles (Glenn Frey, Don Henley and Timothy B. Schmit) contribute backing vocals on the track, and perhaps this was another reason why '21 At 33' peaked higher in the US album chart than anything since 'Blue Moves' four years before, although it was less successful commercially in the UK than 'A Single Man'.

It was, however, rather less commercially successful than another DJM compilation which had been released in the autumn of 1977, 'Greatest Hits Volume II', which somewhat surprisingly included the two biggest Rocket hits, 'Sorry Seems To Be The Hardest Word' and the duet with Kiki Dee, 'Don't Go Breaking My Heart', which, according to Philip Norman's *Elton – The Definitive Biography*, were included at Elton's insistence to avoid 'another substandard compilation'. With a rather fanciful sleeve picture of Elton as a cricketer batting at twilight on a rural ground

Judie Tzuke

in the shadow of a church, this was pretty much what its title suggested – all the hits from 'The Bitch Is Back' to 'Grow Some Funk Of Your Own' plus 'Pinball Wizard' and the first two Rocket hits. The US and UK releases differed slightly – the UK version included 'Bennie And The Jets', which had been on the US version of Elton's first 'Greatest Hits' album, but had been omitted from the British version of the latter because at that time (1974) it had not been a UK hit. By 1977, it had been a hit as a reissue, but it could not be included on the US version of 'Greatest Hits Volume II', as it had already appeared on the US version of the earlier 'Greatest Hits' compilation, and was replaced on the American 'Volume II' by 'Levon' – got that? Although it failed to reach the Top 20 of the US chart, the album was certified platinum, and additionally reached the Top 10 of the UK chart.

The end of 1980 also brought a significant change of label for Elton in the United States. Having previously been associated exclusively with MCA in America for both his DJM and Rocket releases, Elton was successfully wooed by the rich and very fashionable Geffen Records, recently launched by David Geffen, whose career in the music business had been constantly moving upwards from his days as part of the management team of Geffen & (Eliott) Roberts, who oversaw the careers of numerous up and coming stars from Joni Mitchell and Laura Nyro to Neil Young, Jackson Browne and The Eagles. The latter two were among the first acts signed to Asylum

Records, the label founded by Geffen and funded by WEA, today the only remaining big record business conglomerate left in America – Sony (CBS) and MCA are now both Japanese-owned, Polygram and BMG (RCA) are run from Germany (and in Polygram's case, Holland), and EMI still retain British involvement. Asylum was attached to Elektra (the 'E' in WEA) and Elektra founder Jac Holzman's idiosyncratic artist roster was soon marginalised as Geffen signed Joni Mitchell and another hit-making rock band, Jo Jo Gunne, which was mainly comprised of ex-members of Spirit, the acid-rock quintet of the late Sixties. By the late Seventies, Geffen had left Asylum and formed another label, Geffen (to which Joni Mitchell later signed, as did Don Henley of The Eagles).

The plum signing of all time would be the comeback album by John Lennon after his five years of being a house-husband and doting father. Lennon's last live appearance had been with Elton back in 1974, on the night when he and his wife Yoko Ono were reconciled, and it wasn't long before Yoko became pregnant, to Lennon's delight – if Yoko's pregnancy came to a satisfactory end rather than the previous miscarriages she had suffered, he vowed to devote himself to the first five years of the life of the child he craved. Sean Ono Lennon was born in October 1975, and in November, 1980, Lennon's 'Double Fantasy' album was released by Geffen Records. Elton had signed with Geffen for America in late September, Lennon in October, which was an advantage

Above
The Eagles

Right
David Geffen

to all three parties – Geffen could justifiably claim that his label was now one of the majors. Ironically, of course, John Lennon was assassinated shortly afterwards, so that the two star signings were only active labelmates for a few weeks, but that almost certainly meant a lot to Elton.

Bernie Taupin was sufficiently moved by the violent death of a hero who had also been a personal friend to write a lyric on the evening of Lennon's death titled 'Empty Garden (Hey Hey Johnny)' to which Elton would add music, but the song would not be included on Elton's next album, which would again involve several lyricists. This would be Elton's first album for Geffen, after ten years with MCA, the last couple of which had not brought the success for which MCA had hoped when they re-signed Elton in 1974 for the biggest deal ever at that time, $8 million for five albums. Nothing since 'Blue Moves' in 1976 had reached the Top 10, and '21 At 33' was the end of the contract, so why not go with Geffen, particularly if John Lennon (of all people) was also on Geffen!

Background
Open air concert in New York's
Central Park, 1980

The Fox

I Saw Her Standing There

Nobody Wins

Chloe

Breaking Down Barriers

Just Like Belgium

Heart In The Right Place

Fascist Faces

Heels Of The Wind

Fanfare

Carla / Etude

Legal Boys

Blue Eyes

Empty Garden

Dear John

(Hey Hey Johnny)

Ball And Chain

2 Low 4 Zero

I'm Still Standing

I Guess That's Why

Kiss The Bride

They Call It The Blues

Cold As Christmas

(Crystal)

(In The Middle Of The Year)

One More Arrow

Sad Songs (Say So Much)

Who Wears These Shoes

Breaking Hearts

Slow Down Georgie

(Ain't What It Used To Be)

(She's Poison)

Burning Buildings

In Neon

Ice On Fire

Act Of War

This Town

Too Young

Nikita

Wrap Her Up

That's What Friends Are For

I'm Still
Standing

The first record release of 1981 involving Elton was a smart piece of work on someone's part, especially as his last single of 1980, 'Dear God', the heavily choral track from '21 At 33', had been released in Britain (but not in America), and had made little impression. With the murder of John Lennon still fresh in everyone's minds, it was an obvious move for DJM to compile the three tracks recorded at Madison Square Garden six years before on one single, provided EMI (the label to which Lennon was signed at the time) had no objection. Released in March, 1981, the single reached the UK Top 40, but was possibly not released in this form in the US. 'I Saw Her Standing There' was consequently the third John Lennon-related single simultaneously in the UK chart, but the elderly live tracks were no match commercially for 'Imagine' (widely regarded as Lennon's finest song) and 'Woman' (from his 'comeback' album), which both topped the UK singles chart at the start of 1981 as Lennon was remembered much more fondly by record buyers than for much of the previous seven years.

Elton's new album of the year was titled 'The Fox', and this once again involved four collaborators, but this time with James Newton Howard in the place of Judie Tzuke completing the quartet with Taupin, Osborne and Robinson. Tzuke had made much more progress than any of the other Rocket signings of the period, and had actually done rather better than even Kiki Dee by reaching the Top 20 of the UK album chart with each of her first three LPs, 'Welcome To The Cruise' (1979), 'Sports Car' (1980, which reached the Top 10) and 'I Am Phoenix' (1981). Tzuke was arguably the most enduring of all the artists (apart from Elton of course) signed to Rocket. At the end of 1981, her three year contract was up, and she moved to Chrysalis, a very hot label at the time with Blondie, Spandau Ballet, The Specials, Ultravox and so on, which must have been an offer she couldn't refuse, although there is no reason to suppose that she was unhappy with Rocket after three hit albums.

Nineteen eighty-one also saw the label's biggest ever UK hit single by an act other than Elton (alone or duetting with Kiki Dee) – a folk singer/ comedian /entertainer from the west of England with the unlikely name of Fred Wedlock had recorded an amusing song about middle-aged Lotharios titled 'The Oldest Swinger In Town', and somehow Rocket released it, perhaps thinking it might attract radio play as a novelty item and then chart for a couple of weeks. This was a very astute move, as the single almost reached the Top 5 in a respectable chart life of over two months, but it was the last Rocket single not involving Elton to reach the UK Top 20. Rocket had tried for five years to expand its artist roster, but the cost of promotion for credible and worthy, but unfashionable acts like Stackridge, Blue, Alan Hull and others was just too high for the modest sales which resulted. Well after punk rock's brief period at the cutting edge of musical fashion, there was still a stigma attached to being musically adept, and this coincided with the period when Rocket were looking for talent. A number of acts on the label made impressive records, but for almost all of them the timing was wrong.

Ironically, this was also the case for Elton himself. While there had been a few successes since 1976 (most recently with 'Song For Guy'), he was no longer odds on to top the chart, even in the US, where his status had been God-like a few years before. Fate had intervened on several fronts: punk rock had made him seem old-fashioned, his longtime songwriting partner was seemingly wearing his heart on his sleeve rather too noticeably, his producer had left, and Elton's own attempts to explore new musical directions had been only marginally successful; the magic of the first half of the Seventies was only occasionally discernible. It was no one's fault, it just all happened at once. Perhaps the revelation about his bisexuality had caused more harm in America than anyone could have foreseen, but whatever it was, the music no longer seemed consistently brilliant to many long-time fans. Dudgeon's absence was probably crucial to the sound of the records veering (perhaps too far) towards R&B, but the real problem was that Elton was not making records which appealed to his fans.

'The Fox' was a good example of this, failing to reach the Top 20 of the *Billboard* album chart and not selling enough for gold certification, a situation which would have been simply unthinkable a few years earlier, although it did not fare too badly in the British charts, more or less equalling the performance of '21 At 33'. In fact 'The Fox' was far from a disaster in artistc terms, one interesting factor being the return on three tracks of the old faithful rhythm section of Dee Murray and Nigel Olsson, with Murray also playing on a couple of other tracks.

Of the four songs involving Gary Osborne, 'Nobody Wins' was the most commercially successful, becoming a medium sized hit single in the US, and a minor hit in Britain, although curiously the song is not credited to Elton as a songwriter at all, but to Jean-Paul Dreau and Gary Osborne. The song was not a typical vehicle for Elton, sounding much closer to the type of Jacques Brel song as recorded by Scott Walker, while 'Breaking Down Barriers' (with Olsson, Murray and James Newton Howard plus American guitarist Richie Zito) was a reasonable opener for the album. 'Heart In The Right Place', with its staccato rhythm, and Howard on vocoder, seems overlong, while 'Chloe', a minor US hit single, seemed rather low-key. Four lyrics by Bernie Taupin seemed to suggest that he was recovering from his depression, although the strangely titled 'Just Like Belgium', released in the summer of 1981 as a UK single, was a flop, although it is not a sub-standard track by any means. 'Fascist Faces', 'Heels Of The Wind' (with its memorable line 'just a kick away from the heels of the wind') and the title

track, with Mickey Raphael, a longtime part of Willie Nelson's band, on harmonica, all sound impressive, although the precise meaning of their lyrics is uncertain.

The one song on the album written by Elton and Tom Robinson, 'Elton's Song', is a pleasant ballad which was written in 1979, and the centre-piece of the album is a three part track,'Carla/Etude', 'Fanfare' (both instrumentals) and the previously mentioned 'Chloe'. Overall, better than 'Victim Of Love' and the Thom Bell tracks, and no worse than '21 At 33', 'The Fox' certainly deserves a considered re-evaluation.

One other aspect of 'The Fox' which was very worthy of note was that over half the album was produced by Chris Thomas, who would become Elton's regular producer for the first half of the 1980s. Thomas, a musician during the Sixties, had built a strong reputation, initially working as George Martin's assistant, in which capacity he was involved in a good deal of the studio sessions for the 1968 double album by The Beatles (the 'white' album), after which he enjoyed some success with Procol Harum, John Cale and Roxy Music, as well as mixing Pink Floyd's incredibly successful 'Dark Side Of The Moon', which accumulated more weeks on the *Billboard* 'Top 200 Albums' chart than any other LP – nearly five years more than its nearest rival!

In the second half of the 1970s, Thomas had successfully produced The Sex Pistols, The Tom Robinson Band, Paul McCartney's Wings, The Pretenders and Pete Townshend, and was arguably one of the hottest producers in the world in the early 1980s. Typically, he was modest about his work on 'The Fox' when it was suggested to him that he had been hired to 'save' the album, the first half of which had been produced by Elton and Clive Franks: 'It was David Geffen who thought it was a salvage job, but I think Elton himself was pretty pleased with the album when he'd finished it. I did six tracks of the eleven on the album, and I really thought that the ones on the album I didn't do were very good, and probably better than my stuff.'

Coincidentally, Thomas and Elton had both been at the Royal Academy Of Music, and had been there at the same time, although Thomas was a gifted child violinist: 'Of course, I had known Elton before – he had a junior exhibition at the Academy too, although I can't actually remember him from that time.' Where he did remember meeting Elton was when he produced a single of 'The Dick Barton Theme' for something called The Bread And Beer Band: 'That was at a time when we were both trying to get something going for ourselves, when he was a session musician. He knew various people at Air [Studios], and dreamed up various mad ideas, or they would find a solo singer and ask me to produce them, and Elton would get a backing band together which would usually include Caleb Quaye and Roger Pope, and there were always those ties because of the relationship between Dick James and Air ' [George Martin, who was a partner in Air Studios, was obviously very friendly with Dick James, the only publisher interested in taking on The Beatles when they were virtually unknown outside Liverpool and Hamburg]. Thomas didn't say whether Elton had hired him because of their shared past, but it's likely that this was a consideration.

Obviously, Elton was pleased about the working reunion, because Thomas was also hired to do the next album, 1982's 'Jump Up', which not only restored Elton to the ranks of gold certified artists, but also returned him to the Top 20 of the US album chart. In the UK, Elton had not released a Top 10 album since 1978, and 'Jump Up' was not the album to end that absence, although like '21 At 33' and 'The Fox', it almost reached the Top 10 in a three month spell in the chart. Like them, it included two hit singles, but the curious thing about 'Jump Up' is that both singles are in the second half of the album, which seems far more interesting than the first five tracks. This time it was five tracks with Taupin, four with Osborne and one with Tim Rice, who at the time may well have been estranged from his tunesmith partner, Andrew Lloyd Webber. Rice had two massive musicals behind him written with Lloyd Webber, *Jesus Christ Superstar* and *Evita*, which had included several major hit singles, and their success had elevated Rice & Lloyd Webber to the heights of a theatrical Lennon & McCartney.

Unfortunately, 'Legal Boys' sounds very like a then-typical Tim Rice show number, and not especially appropriate for Elton, although their partnership would win an Academy Award in the 1990s for the soundtrack of the Walt Disney cartoon feature film *The Lion King*. Rice later recalled meeting Elton in 1971. 'He was with US Decca (MCA) in those days, and so were A.Lloyd Webber and I. I recall being extremely narked that we had to share the front cover of *Cashbox* with Elton one week that year – no doubt he felt equally peeved. My beef was however more justified

Blue Eyes

as we have never got onto the front cover again, and EJ has made many returns to this coveted position in all the trade magazines. Maybe my minor contribution to his new album will change my luck in that respect.'

The first UK single was a song co-written by Gary Osborne, 'Blue Eyes', a languid Sinatra-esque ballad which became Elton's first UK Top 10 hit of the 1980s, and in fact his first to reach those heights since 'Song For Guy' in 1978. In the US, it was decided to release as the first single from the album the far weightier 'Empty Garden (Hey Hey Johnny)', the song for which Bernie Taupin had written the lyrics on the day after John Lennon was murdered. As he says in the song, 'a gardener like that one, no one can replace', and this is a very sincere tribute, which was a US Top 20 hit when it was released there before 'Blue Eyes', which also almost reached the US Top 10.

It was a different story in Britain, where 'Blue Eyes' had been a big success, but 'Empty Garden' peaked just outside the Top 50. Its brief spell in the chart was at a time when the Number One hits were Adam Ant's 'Goody Two Shoes', Charlene's 'I've Never Been To Me' and Captain Sensible's 'Happy Talk', so perhaps the national mood was not conducive to a classy tribute . . .

Another track on the album, 'Dear John', co-written by Gary Osborne, is nothing to do with John Lennon, but is a rocker about the end of a relationship, while another song involving Osborne, the cheerful country-inclined 'Ball And Chain', has Pete Townshend guesting on guitar. A third John/Osborne song, 'Princess', is a melodious love song, although

2 Low 4 Zero

the five Taupin songs other than 'Empty Garden' generally seem only averagely inspired. However, this was his biggest contribution since 'Blue Moves' six years earlier, and it seemed he was definitely on the way back, although few would have expected that only a year later, he would write the complete lyrics for what is without doubt one of Elton's finest albums of the 1980s, 'Too Low For Zero', on which the original band of Elton, Dee Murray, Nigel Olsson and Davey Johnstone reunited after an eight year gap, although Johnstone, Olsson and Murray had all worked sporadically with Elton during that time, but rarely, if ever, all together.

The reaction to this album on opposite sides of the Atlantic was diverse, to say the least; in the UK, it was not only his first Top 10 album for close on five years, it was his first new album for ten years to remain in the chart for over six months, and ultimately it was listed for well over a year. Clearly, this was a comeback of the type which would have seemed very unlikely, if not impossible, at the time of 'Victim Of Love'. In America, the album also hung around in the chart for longer than anything since 'Caribou', but it didn't even reach the Top 20 of the *Billboard* chart, and peaked lower than any of Elton's albums apart from the 'Friends' soundtrack, 'The Thom Bell Sessions' and 'Victim Of Love'. The three albums which dominated the US album chart during that period were Michael Jackson's 'Thriller', 'Synchronicity' by The Police and the soundtrack album to the *Footloose* movie, and compared to Michael

Jackson and Sting particularly, Elton John was definitely yesterday's news, although it is still difficult to understand how America in general was apparently suffering from a nationwide attack of deafness, because 'Too Low' was (and is) a very impressive album.

In artistic terms, 'Too Low For Zero' was a renaissance for Elton, not only because his old band and his songwriting partner were working with him again, but even the look of the sleeve was more up to date, with a clever graphic representing the four words in the title. Not only that, the songs were far stronger than anything since the mid-Seventies, and included four UK hit singles, and even three which reached the *Billboard* Top 40.

Once again, singles were released in a different order on opposite sides of the Atlantic: in the UK, the first hit from the album was the irresistibly melodic 'I Guess That's Why They Call It The Blues', on which Stevie Wonder contributed an instantly identifiable harmonica solo which doubtless helped to propel Elton into the Top 5 of the singles chart for the first time since 'Song For Guy' five years before. This was the only track on which another song writer, Davey Johnstone, was credited besides Elton and Bernie, and all the other nine tracks were solely written by the established team.

The first single from the album in the US was a similarly great song, but with an additional poignancy in its lyrics: 'I'm Still Standing' is a joyful celebration, with Elton singing 'I'm still standing better than I ever did, Lookin' like a true survivor, feelin' like a

Left
Stevie Wonder

little kid'. Elton found it enjoyable to sing, especially because he was experiencing some with his American record company, Geffen, and defiantly addressed it to them. Whether that turn of events contributed to its failure to become hit single in the US is something we can only guess at.

It also features a good Davey Johnstone guitar solo, and the song has remained virtually Elton's signature tune. It is hard to understand how it failed to become a US Top 10 hit as the first single from Elton's best album in years, but in the UK, where it was the follow-up single to 'I Guess That's Why They Call It The Blues', it became his second Top 5 single in three months, something he had not achieved since the 'Yellow Brick Road' era.

But it didn't end there – the second US single and third UK single was 'Kiss The Bride', with an unforgettable riff following the singing of the title phrase. This was a slightly smaller hit (US Top 30, UK Top 20), but was no doubt hampered from rising higher in the singles charts by the fact that many fans already owned the album, which was probably also true of 'Cold As Christmas (In The Middle Of The Year)', a ballad on which Kiki Dee assisted vocally, which, unsurprisingly, was released as a fourth UK single at Christmas, 1983, when it became a Top 40 hit. In the States, 'I Guess That's Why They Call It The Blues' was finally released as the third single from the album, and became Elton's first Top 5 hit since 'Little Jeanie'. Several other tracks on the album were equally excellent, such as the fast-paced 'Crystal', where Elton sings the words so fast that a look at the lyric sheet is necessary to have any idea of the subject matter, or the

final track, which was orchestrated by James Newton Howard, 'One More Arrow'.

There can be little doubt about the major reason for this somewhat overdue return to top form, which was that Elton and Bernie Taupin were back in harness at last. Even more significantly, they both had embarked on new relationships, Taupin with an American named Toni Russo, whom he married in 1979, and who, according to Philip Norman's book helped Bernie reassemble his life, and to whom he dedicated the 'Too Low For Zero' album. Rather more surprisingly, Elton also found a girl friend, a German lady named Renate Blauel, who was working at Air Studios as a recording engineer when the album was being finally mixed, and to whom Elton took a strong liking. She was given a name-check on 'Too Low For Zero', although her involvement in the album had apparently only started as it was being finally completed.

Bernie Taupin regarded the 'Too Low For Zero' album as another milestone, because it marked their reunion as a full-time team after a couple of years of only sporadic collaboration, and the 'Too Low' project was a return to 100% commitment. The major reason for their separation had been purely geographical, and both partners were at pains to emphasise that they had never ever fallen out or been involved in a serious argument, and Elton called the hiatus 'a healthy time apart', intimating that had they not diversified as they did, a permanent split might have resulted. Whatever either did during their estrangement, there can be no doubt that as individuals, no matter who their collaborators were, the results were almost always less spectacular than those that had

been consistently achieved by their long standing union; and this is no reflection on such major names as Tim Rice, Alice Cooper or Rod Stewart, the separation was simply perfect proof of the adage about the whole (Elton & Bernie working together) being greater than the sum of the parts. For the next Elton John album, 1984's 'Breaking Hearts', Renate was much more involved, and was credited on the LP as engineer.

Meanwhile, Watford Football Club had justified Elton's faith and investment by going from strength to strength. The 1982/83 season found them in the First Division for the very first time in their history. It was disclosed that Elton had provided over £1 million in interest-free loans to the club, which had now become one of the most successful in Britain. In their first season in Division One, Watford ended up placed second to the top, a considerable achievement which meant that they had also qualified to play in the very lucrative UEFA Cup, a pan-European competition.

During the summer of 1983, Elton had travelled with the Watford team to China, where they played three games against local opposition, and he also accompanied his team to Germany for their first European match, although unfortunately Watford lost. But their second season in Division One, 1983/84, was still tinged with glory, as Watford reached the F.A.Cup Final for the first time ever, although once again they came second, beaten by Everton, as Elton, with Renate, watched. Elton called watching that Cup Final 'the happiest day of my life', although he qualified his delight by adding 'other than getting married, of course'.

Above
Elton and the Watford FC squad for the 1982/83 season

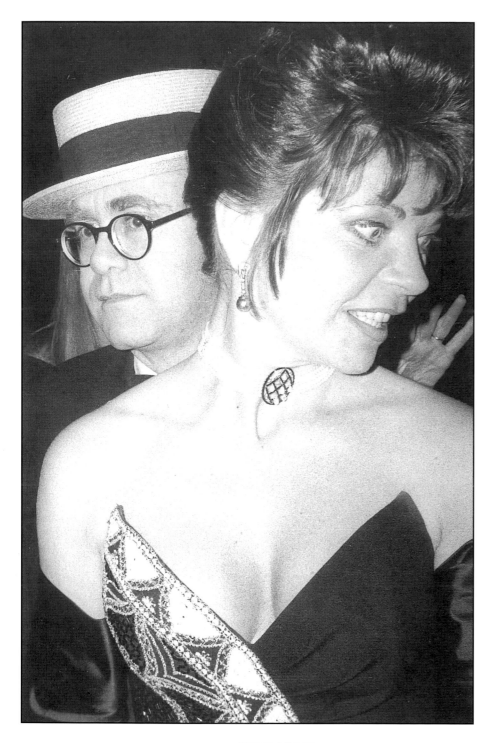

Elton and Renata

Three months before Watford went to Wembley Stadium (where Elton had appeared as a performer), he and Renate were married on February 14th, 1984 (St.Valentine's Day, appropriately) in Australia after having known each other a matter of months rather than years. One of Elton's main motivations was the desire for a family – his mother apparently bought the couple a perambulator in the expectation of soon becoming a grandmother. The album Renate engineered, with Chris Thomas again producing, was certainly comparable in quality to 'Too Low For Zero', and 'Breaking Hearts' reached the UK Top 3, Elton's first album to aspire to such heights since 'Blue Moves', although in America it was his fourth consecutive Top 20 album, despite including three US Top 40 hits, one of which took him into the US Top 3 for the first time since 1980. With four UK hit singles, two of which went Top 10, this showed that Elton and the record-buying public were again seeing eye to eye.

Five of the ten tracks on the album were hits – 'Sad Songs (Say So Much)', which was in the same approximate style as 'I Guess That's Why They Call It The Blues', was a US Top 3/UK Top 10 hit. This was a more upbeat song than its title suggested, as was 'Passengers', an infectious song which was a UK Top 5 hit, and was apparently a Taupin comment on apartheid, a *cause célèbre* at that time. Next came 'Who Wears These Shoes', a song in which the protagonist seemingly wants to know the identity of the person who has replaced him (or her), which was far more successful in the US, where it made the Top 20, than in Britain, where it briefly crept into the Top 50. Even this fared better in UK chart terms than the album's title track, 'Breaking Hearts (Ain't What It Used To Be)', a melodic ballad with a resigned air and an introduction reminiscent of Randy Newman. This was released to coincide with Elton's first wedding anniversary, but with Britain in the grip of Frankie Goes To Hollywood's 'Relax' and Nena's '99 Red Balloons', a melodic ballad was somewhat at odds with prevailing musical trends. In the US, the UK B-side of 'Breaking Hearts' was released in the US as an A-side, which reached the Top 40, and the track in question, 'In Neon' is arguably a more adventurous song than 'Breaking Hearts'.

Once again, there was plenty more in the way of notable tracks on the album apart those released as singles, including the presumably allegorical 'Burning Buildings' and the bouncy 'Slow Down Georgie (She's Poison)', with its brilliant couplet 'the reputation of the woman you're dating's about as nasty as the Berlin wall'. Altogether, a fine album, which seemed to prove that the 'back to basics' policy with Taupin as lyricist and the Johnstone/Murray/Olsson trio was working well, but curiously it was not pursued on the 1985 album, 'Ice On Fire'. In fact, this album did not appear until the end of that year, during which Elton was busy with other projects.

Elton had either been out of the country (most likely) or was simply not invited (a ridiculous oversight if true) to participate in the multi-million selling Band Aid charity single, 'Do They Know It's Christmas', but when it came to Live Aid, the all-day concert in London and New York on July 13th, 1985, Elton was an obvious choice to perform, and

for many, the highlight of his appearance was his show-stopping duet with George Michael. The latter had just disbanded Wham!, the very popular and successful duo of himself and Andrew Ridgeley, after a spectacular farewell concert at Wembley Stadium just two weeks earlier, in which Elton had duetted with Michael on 'Candle In The Wind'.

Elton had encountered George Michael, clearly the strength behind Wham! as lead vocalist and songwriter, on March 13, 1985, when he presented Michael with an Ivor Novello Award as Best Songwriter; Elton referred to Michael as 'a major songwriter in the tradition of Paul McCartney and Barry Gibb'. This was the start of something of a mutual appreciation society between two huge stars which would continue on Elton's next album. At Live Aid, Elton and Michael duetted on 'Don't Let The Sun Go Down On Me' after Elton had performed 'I'm Still Standing', 'Bennie &The Jets', 'Rocket Man' and 'Don't Go Breaking My Heart' (with Kiki Dee). Live Aid's initial inspiration and prime organiser Bob Geldof later said of Elton: 'His music obviously speaks for itself, but personally he is one of the kindest people I have ever met, and certainly one of the bravest.'

For reasons which remain vague, neither Dee Murray nor Nigel Olsson had been invited to work in the band during the promotional tour following the release of the 'Breaking Hearts' album, and when it was time to record the follow-up album, they did not participate, although Davey Johnstone was still involved. Another absentee was producer Chris Thomas, who had helped to revive Elton's career with two worthy albums, but this time,

The Live Aid concert at Wembley Stadium, London. 13th July 1985

Elton back stage with Freddie Mercury at the Live Aid Concert

Act Of War

Gus Dudgeon was invited to produce Elton once again. One convenient aspect of this arrangement was that Dudgeon had bought a recording studio at Cookham in Berkshire, within easy reach of Elton's house at Windsor, although Renate, of course, was not the recording engineer.

The album was titled 'Ice On Fire', using a phrase in the song 'Nikita', which appeared to be about falling in love with someone on the Soviet side of the Berlin Wall. This melodic ballad was ultimately the biggest single from the album, although it was not the first hit on either side of the Atlantic. Why it was decided to release 'Act Of War' as the first single from 'Ice On Fire' can only be guessed at; this was a fairly spectacular duet between Elton and Millie Jackson, an American soul star noted for what *The Penguin Encyclopedia Of Popular Music* describes as her 'stage act marked by four letter words, (and her) attempt at ultra-raunchy image'. Apparently, the part Jackson played was initially offered to Tina Turner, who turned it down. Elton and Mille Jackson had performed the song at the Montreux Rock Festival earlier that year, and although the idea was quite good, the song obviously failed to connect with audiences, and peaked outside the UK Top 30 around the time of Live Aid.

In the autumn, when things had returned to normal after the excitement of the Wembley shows that summer, 'Nikita', which featured George Michael (by this time, the biggest star in the UK pop firmament) as a backing vocalist and another big star of the moment, Nik Kershaw, who played guitar on the track, was released as a UK single, which reached the Top 10. Kershaw had accumulated five UK Top

10 singles in 18 months, the biggest of which was titled 'I Won't Let The Sun Go Down On Me' (very reminiscent of Elton's 'Don't Let The Sun Go Down On Me' lyrically, if taken at a faster tempo). The rhythm section on this track (and several others on the album) was also new to Elton, with Fairport Convention drummer Dave Mattacks and David Paton, one of the leaders of the briefly successful Scottish pop band, Pilot, on bass.

The rhythm section of John Deacon on bass and Roger Taylor on drums, which played on the next track, 'Too Young', was even better known as the rhythm section of Queen, a group John Reid had briefly managed at a time in the late Seventies when Elton had announced his intention of temporarily retiring from touring. The demands on one manager which might accrue from simultaneously representing two such celebrities as Elton and Freddie Mercury (not to mention Mercury's colleagues) were clearly an impossible task, and when Elton returned, Queen found another manager.

'Nikita' was not released as a US single until the start of 1986, when it equalled its achievement in Britain by reaching the Top 10. Other guest stars also appeared on the 'Ice On Fire' album – Sister Sledge, the American vocal quartet who are actually sisters and who sold a million copies of their 1979 single, 'We Are Family', appeared as backing vocalists on the opening track, 'This Town', along with yet another rhythm section, drummer Charlie Morgan and bass player Paul Westwood, who had both worked with Nik Kershaw, while keyboard player Fred Mandel had played in Queen's backing band. This trio also played

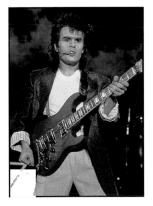

Nik Kershaw

Left
Elton and Millie Jackson duet on 'Act of War', 1985

Sister Sledge

on 'Cry To Heaven', a rather mournful song about a country at war, which was possibly motivated by the situation in Northern Ireland.

The other single from 'Ice On Fire' was 'Wrap Her Up', a strange track which nevertheless was a Top 20 hit on both sides of the Atlantic. The song featured George Michael and Elton both singing, although it was less a duet than a call and response item, in which at one point a long succession of females were namechecked, including Marlene Dietrich, Marilyn Monroe, Samantha Fox, Brigitte Bardot, Shirley Temple, Nancy Reagan (!), Linda Lovelace (star of the infamous porn movie *Deep Throat*), Elsie Tanner (a character from the television soap opera *Coronation Street*) and Annie Lennox. This was undeniably a novelty song, and possibly not even to be taken completely seriously, although one should never forget the stunning success achieved by 'Bennie & The Jets', which is arguably similar in style.

According to Gus Dudgeon, 'Shoot Down The Moon', a wistful and rather anguished song on which the only other musicians apart from Elton himself were Fred Mandel playing synthesiser and Pino Palladino on bass, was written because Elton decided that he wanted to write the theme tune for a James Bond movie, but eventually the film's producers used A View To A Kill by Duran Duran. The most obvious personal observation to be made after re-listening to the 'Ice On Fire' album is that Elton seems to work better with a quartet than in a ten piece band.

If 'Ice On Fire' wasn't a bad album, it was certainly not an obvious improvement on 'Breaking Hearts', and Dudgeon's return

seemed to point to the fact that his working relationship with Elton had understandably changed since 1976. However, Elton was involved in a massive hit single at the end of 1985. The great Dionne Warwick organised and led an all-star quartet credited as Dionne & Friends, her colleagues Elton, Stevie Wonder and Gladys Knight, in a song about Aids awareness, 'That's What Friends Are For', which was Elton's first appearance at the top of the Billboard Hot 100 since 1976. It topped the US chart for a month, but didn't quite make the UK Top 10.

There were other things exercising the minds of Elton and those around him, as Elton was sueing Dick James for the return of the copyright in his songs, because of miscalculation of songwriting royalties relating to sub-publishing agreements – it was said that Elton had been cheated of £1 million! This saga would be resolved to no one's complete satisfaction at the end of the year. Another change in Elton's activities would occur in 1986, when his relationship with Watford FC, whom he had greatly assisted to become a major force, began to change with the departure of Graham Taylor, who felt that after ten years as manager of the club, it was time for a change. A few years later, Elton obviously came to a similar conclusion.

Left
Elton and Sir John Gielgud
Christmas 1984

Leather *Jackets* Ang*eline*

Heartache *All Over The World* That's What *Friends Are For*

Slow *Rivers* Memory *Of Love*

I Fall *Apart*

Don't Trust *That Woman* **Hoop** *Of Fire*

Go It *Alone* *Flames Of Paradise*

Greatest Hits *Volume 3*

Live *In Australia* Candle *In The Wind*

The Greatest *Discovery* **Tiny** *Dancer* To*night* **Blue** *Moves*

Madman *Across The Water* Sorry Seems To Be

The Hardest Word

Don't Go Breaking *My heart*

Have Mercy *On The Criminal* **Burn Down** *The Mission*

I Don't Wanna *Go On With You Like That* Town Of *Plenty*

Reg *Strikes Back* A Word *In Spanish*

Goodbye *Marlon Brando* Mona Lisas *And Mad Hatters*

Since God *Invented Girls* Heavy *Traffic* The Camera *Never Lies*

The *Rumour* Through *The Storm* Healing *Hands*

Sleeping With *The Past*

Club At The End *Of The Street* Durban *Deep* **Sa***crifice*

You Gotta Love *Someone* I Never Knew *Her Name*

The Very Best *Of Elton John*

Donner Pour *Donner* Come Back *Baby* I Feel *Like A Bullet*

To Be *Continued . . .*

Easier To *Walk Away*

1986

Sacrifice

1990

Sa*crifice*

Released in the autumn of 1985, 'That's What Friends Are For' became Elton's first landmark of 1986 and marked the beginning of a personal crusade against Aids. The song had originally been contributed to the 1982 film *Night Shift* by the (then) husband-and-wife team of Burt Bacharach & Carole Bayer Sager. Performed in that instance by Rod Stewart, it failed to find release as a single because, said Sager, 'the record company thought it was too soft'. Its theme lent itself perfectly to the cause and, originally conceived by Sager as a duet between Dionne Warwick and Stevie Wonder, it was expanded to take in Gladys Knight. But to its writer's ears, at least, there was still something missing: 'It still needed one more singer, one more punch at the end for that final chorus.'

The suggestion to call Elton came from Clive Davis, head of Warwick's label, Arista, who had also okayed the donation of the record company's profit share to AmFar (the American Foundation for Aids Research). For his part, Elton had been happy to lend his name and talents to the cause. 'I've lost more people to this disease than any other,' he later told BBC Radio. 'That's What Friends Are For' followed the similarly charitable USA For Africa's 'We Are The World' in topping the US singles chart, thereby raising large sums for a worthy cause. It also registered the seventh occasion on which Elton had achieved the US singles chart summit (the last, little short of a decade earlier, had also been a shared credit, with Kiki Dee on 'Don't Go Breaking My Heart'). In Britain, 'That's What Friends Are For' reached the Top 20, making it little more than a moderate success.

January 1986 also saw the final resolution of the dispute over royalties with Dick James Music that had first come to court in June 1985. Elton and Bernie Taupin had claimed back the copyrights to 136 songs written between 1967 and 1973, a body of work that included 'Rocket Man', 'Crocodile Rock' and many more of his biggest hits and a catalogue that had reputedly already grossed some £200 million. The claim was that Elton had been naive when he signed to DJM, that he had sought no independent legal advice because he had trusted Dick James implicitly, and that DJM had consciously concealed from Elton and Bernie the workings of a network of overseas publishing affiliates that had diminished his earnings considerably. There had certainly been an element of trust: Dick James, after all, had been the publisher of the many familiar songs written by The Beatles, and the man who had co-founded Northern Songs with John Lennon, Paul McCartney and the Beatles' manager Brian Epstein.

'It was a very exciting period,' Elton told the court of his earliest days as a writer, emphasising that he was very young. 'The basic points of the contract had been pointed out, and in all good faith I just signed it.' Both John and Taupin had obtained the consent of their parents before signing, but, said Elton: 'I did not think about going to a solicitor. I just

trusted Mr James. Their terms seemed very fair to us at the time. Anything anyone told me, I believed.' The stakes were high: if Elton lost, costs could comfortably exceed £1 million, but the value of the catalogue could be up to 30 times greater. It was a calculated risk, and one that had implications for the whole world of music publishing: Stephen James (son of Dick James) went so far as to claim, somewhat melodramatically, that if Elton won, 'the music business is finished'.

The terms the duo had been offered had not been overly generous, but then many artists of the time probably signed similar contracts. The record deal had been renegotiated in 1970, the breakthrough year with the 'Elton John' LP, increasing the royalty rate from around two per cent of retail price to four and then six per cent. DJM had also signed Elton to a five-year management deal, arguably a conflict of interest, especially as Elton had not sought independent legal advice at the time. Elton was present at most of the trial, but not for the judgement, which happened to coincide with a live engagement in Edinburgh; Bernie Taupin, however, had flown in from Beverley Hills to be present.

The case ended in November 1985, after more than fifty days in court, the complex, four-hour judgement being delivered in December. Elton had, it was decided, suffered under the 'dominating influence' of Dick James, but the gap between the signing and the writ had been unduly long. Also, since DJM had invested much time and money in breaking Elton worldwide, it was reasonable for them to expect a certain reward for their risk-taking. The judge decreed that the duo should be compensated for concealment of royalties from their overseas sales, but their copyrights or master recordings were not returned to them. 'The industry consensus,' said one observer, 'was that Elton John won a battle, and perhaps several moral victories, but he ultimately lost the war.'

If that was so, consolation came at the end of January with the award of £5 million in back royalties: this had been the sum the John and Taupin team had been expecting, although DJM apparently believed it might be around a tenth of the figure. Just days afterwards, on February 4th, Dick James died from a heart attack. That same month, the *Daily Telegraph* reported that Elton was going to meet his late publisher's sizeable legal bill on the court case, laying to rest with grace a legal battle that had lasted too long. Within a year, another bonanza for the legal profession – and one far more potentially damaging to Elton's career – would begin.

Even the highs seemed to have their dark side: when Elton was honoured for his Outstanding Contribution To British Music at the music industry's fifth annual BRIT Awards, he reportedly said that he would never attend such a self-congratulatory event again after he had received his award from right wing Conservative MP Norman Tebbit – it is not suggested that his disapproval was chiefly about his presenter, a man whose views were often regarded as too Thatcherite for comfort, but his questioning of the very concept of such back-slapping jamborees and his dry comment that 'it makes good television' left little doubt that the event itself had more or less left him cold.

Elton receiving the award for Outstanding Contribution To British Music from Conservative MP Norman Tebbit, 1986

This was a view with which many in the UK record industry sympathised. It had indeed been a curious accolade, since the visit to Russia it apparently commemorated had taken place seven years previously. As 'Nikita' hit the US Top 10 in March, 'Cry To Heaven' was peaking just inside the UK Top 50, despite a prime time plug on BBC-TV's Wogan. Considerable consolation came on April 7th, however, when 'Nikita' was voted Best Song Musically And Lyrically at the 31st annual Ivor Novello Awards, held at London's Grosvenor House Hotel. Elton was also honoured with an award for his Outstanding Contribution To British Music.

It was doubtful whether the odd five million from the DJM case would make an appreciable difference to Elton's bank account, let alone his lifestyle, but his willingness to work for charity continued. June 1986 saw him star in the first concerts by the Prince's Trust, an organisation fronted by the Prince of Wales, to celebrate the charity's tenth birthday. Elton, who performed 'I'm Still Standing', shared the limelight with Bryan Adams, Eric Clapton and Tina Turner, before commencing a US tour in August. Before that, he appeared on TV's *The Tube* in July interviewed by Paula Yates . Later that month, Elton and Renate were guests at the wedding of Prince Andrew and Sarah Ferguson, whose friendship, it was said, had helped Elton and his wife through some difficult times. It was also time for a new album to catch the Christmas sales tide, and this would duly appear in October. The single that previewed it was 'Heartache All Over The World', and again its chart performance proved disappointing: it just about reached the Top 50 in

Britain but, in the US, was Elton's smallest hit since 'Border Song' in 1970, peaking outside the Top 50 of the *Billboard* singles chart.

Similarly, 'Leather Jackets', the album from which 'Heartaches' had been excerpted, proved a commercial flop in barely reaching the Top 100 of the US album chart, far and away his worst-performing release there, making 'Victim Of Love' seem like a positive triumph, while its peak position just outside the Top 20 of the UK chart was rather more respectable. Gus Dudgeon had again produced the album, his credit thanking everyone involved for 'the good times, long hours and hard work!'; the recording venue was Hilversum in Holland, where the state-of-the-art Wisseloord Studio complex was situated. The musician credits for 'Leather Jackets' included regulars old and new like Davey Johnstone, David Paton, Charlie Morgan and Fred Mandel, plus Dave Mattacks and Paul Westwood occasionally deputising on drums and bass respectively. Elsewhere, the album's cast list included guests such as Queen's rhythm section of John Deacon and Roger Taylor, who again appeared on one track, 'Angeline', although their contribution was recorded at Dudgeon's Sol Studios in Berkshire, many miles from Wisseloord, while the ever-faithful Kiki Dee helped out as backing vocalist with Shirley Lewis, the sister of mid-Seventies hitmaker Linda Lewis.

The past duets with George Michael were to some extent duplicated when Elton invited another guest, Cliff Richard, to sing on the stately 'Slow Rivers'. The other ballads, such as 'Memory Of Love' (the only Gary Osborne lyric on the album) and the stark, intensely

personal, final track, 'I Fall Apart', took up nearly half the album. Of the uptempo tracks, the most effective was 'Don't Trust That Woman', the lyrics to which were supplied by Cher. The writing credits were as unusual as some of the lyrics: 'Cher/Lady Choc Ice'.

Elsewhere, 'Hoop Of Fire' was creditably soulful, offering potential for a cover from a diva of the stature of a Tina Turner or an Aretha Franklin , while 'Go It Alone' and 'Angeline' both showed a heavy contemporary black music influence. The latter was a three-way co-write by Elton, Taupin and Alan Carvell, a vocalist who had toured as part of the 'Ice on Fire' live band and whose name was also found in the backing vocal chorus. If his contribution had been, as one assumes, on the lyrics side, it was rather peripheral: 'Let me use you like a sex machine, talk real dirty and I'll make you scream' was hardly great poetry . . . Like many of Elton's 1980s albums, 'Leather Jackets' was a veritable mixed bag, rather inconsistent in standard and overall mood. Gus Dudgeon's production added a glossy sheen, but it would be difficult to find too many candidates on 'Leather Jackets' for inclusion in any 'Best Of' compilation.

In the circumstances, perhaps it wasn't surprising that the decision was made to revisit the past with a live LP, to be recorded in Australia during a 27-date tour that began in early November 1986. A 13-piece band would provide the musical fireworks, while the Melbourne Symphony Orchestra would be conducted by a familiar Elton associate, James Newton Howard. Elton had undertaken this project with his commercial standing in some disarray, but, as ever, he seemed to

Opposite
Australia, 1986

flourish in the depths of adversity. It seemed he was determined to silence the critics with a display of showmanship that saw him attired in his most outrageous costumes for ages, while the repertoire he performed onstage during the live recording came predominantly from the previous decade.

The first part of the concert featured a 90-minute set from Elton and band, with Mohican and Tina Turner wigs being brought into play. Then, after the rear section of the stage had been drawn back to reveal the 88-piece orchestra in all its splendour, he returned as a bewigged, frock-coated and beauty-spotted 'Amadeus' to play, if not classical music, a selection of his own classics that inevitably and deservedly won rapturous applause. It was this second half of the show that would go on to provide the material for the 14-track album, which would be released as performed 'with absolutely no overdubs'.

The concert, on the final night of the tour, December 14th, was broadcast live by ABC television to 10 million Australian viewers, the country's largest TV audience ever, yet only five days before this most high-profile of events, Elton had collapsed mid-performance in Sydney, an event that attracted worldwide headlines. A sore throat had been the problem and, as Gus Dudgeon put it, he had been 'knee deep in Kleenexes' during the tour.

Below
Elton and the Melbourne Symphony Orchestra broadcast live on Australian television, December 1986

Right
Elton as Tina Turner in Australia, 1986

Left
Elton dressed in one of the 'Amadeus' style costumes Australia 1986

Australia, 1986

Christmas morning saw Elton linking via satellite with Cliff Richard to perform 'Slow Rivers' (the new single which, surprisingly given their joint followings, would peak outside the UK Top 40), while three days later, England's cricket victory in the third Test Match at Sydney saw Elton splashing champagne around the England dressing room. Elton was a big fan of Ian Botham, the English cricketer who many felt was one of the most charismatic player of the era. Botham was compared by Elton to John Lennon for his generosity, *joie de vivre*, his ability to do something outrageous (but foolish) and his kindness, while his cricketing talent was inevitably praised.

Yet despite attempts to put a brave face on things, January 5th, 1987, would find Elton in a hospital bed, preparing for throat surgery. All concerts for 1987 were cancelled as he concentrated on rest and recovery. A biopsy indicated that the lesion doctors removed had been non-malignant, but a rest from live performance was clearly a sensible precaution.

And that wasn't the only break: two months later, Elton and Renate announced that they would separate. Renate left Woodside, their house in Windsor, for a London flat, though Elton claimed the marriage was not over. They remained friends, he confirmed, although he felt a sense of relief that he would no longer be 'living a lie', as he put it. Apart from the obvious sexual aspects of their unlikely (by all accounts) marriage, there remains the question of why one of the biggest superstars of all time chose to marry a recording studio assistant, and one answer may be that Renate was one of the very few people Elton encountered who was not impressed by who he was and what he had achieved, but simply liked him as a human being. Remembering his enjoyment of early days as a Watford director, when he was so pleased to mix with average joes and men in the street, the Renate episode is more explicable, although whisperings that she was no more than a receptacle for a new generation of Eltons seemed too preposterous for words!

On February 24th, Elton received a boost in the shape of his first ever Grammy Award for Best Pop Performance By A Duo Or Group With Vocal which he shared with Dionne Warwick, Gladys Knight and Stevie Wonder, his co-vocalists on the previous year's 'That's What Friends Are For'. Two months later, Elton appeared at an Aids benefit show in London, with his voice seemingly on the mend.

Nineteen eighty seven was the year when he celebrated his 40th birthday. 'I've been bogged down with Elton John,' he grumbled, 'and bogged down with Watford. 'Bennie and the Jets'? I vomit at the thought of it. It's time for a metamorphosis. I've got to shed another skin.' Among the projects at the back of his mind which he said he intended to bring to the foreground were an album of instrumentals and another of cover versions (both items he claimed he'd 'been talking about for so long'), but neither had become reality by 1995. There were pressing personal reasons why his creative process was less than active, and 1987 would not be remembered for its musical content: more than anything else, it would be remembered as the year when the *Sun*, Britain's top-selling tabloid newspaper, set out to crucify Elton John – and failed.

'Elton In Vice Boys Scandal', the headline of February 25th, 1987, was the first of several stories which inspired numerous writs from the singer during the middle of the year. Many would have advised caution, but Elton was set to make this a *cause célèbre*. Innumerable friends, colleagues and other acquaintances warned Elton that he was taking on an opponent who would have many advantages and far more experience of litigation of this type, but to his great credit, Elton treated the allegations as a totally unjustified personal affront, and because he was certain he was in the right, was prepared to go to the wire to prove his innocence. No less a star than Mick Jagger apparently advised Elton to consider all the possible consequences very carefully, but did not go as far as to suggest he just throw in the towel. Elton thought the *Sun* were 'surprised' that he refused to capitulate.

The actual allegations, none of which were proven, seemed to become more and more bizarre, the headlines more and more hurtful. The *Daily Mirror*, arch-rival of the *Sun*, lined up on Elton's side, calling its competitor's orgy revelations 'a lie'. The *Sun* then retaliated by telling its readers to watch Elton's appearance on Michael Parkinson's TV show on April 18th. 'If you believe Elton,' it said with its usual subtlety, 'you'll believe in fairies.' As for Parkinson, 'I believed him, and I hope the viewers did too. In fact, I thought he was bloody marvellous, considering the pressure he is under.' Meanwhile, Elton used the *Daily Mirror* as his own soapbox to tabloid readers: 'My voice is fine; about two months after my operation I was very frightened I wouldn't get any falsettos: I think that in timbre my voice

Live In Australia

has gone down in pitch.' He had, happily, regained his falsetto, but planned to give it a year's rest. 'You helped the nation keep firmly on my side, and I'm very grateful for that,' he said of the *Daily Mirror* investigations which set out to disprove certain *Sun* allegations. 'It's been horrible, but now I'm back.' As it happened, he was being a little premature. In September, the *Sun* would allege he was being investigated for keeping Rottweiler dogs with their voice boxes removed.

Press attention, both for and against, continued to be intense, and when a listening device was found in the bar of a Los Angeles hotel where he was staying, Elton was totally freaked out. His understandable paranoia was fuelled by such events, to the point where he was unsure who he could trust, especially as he had been investigated so publicly and painfully. He genuinely could not understand the reasons behind the seemingly unprovoked attack, especially as his bisexuality was no secret, having been revealed in the previous decade. This lack of comprehension had led to extreme depression and far from typical long spells as a couch (or bed) potato, but Elton's impressive resolve did not weaken.

Happily, by Christmas Elton would find himself vindicated. Meanwhile, though he was musically inactive on doctor's orders, his reputation as a duet specialist had received a further boost when Jennifer Rush, an American who had found fame two years earlier through a German Euro-production of 'The Power Of Love', a pseudo-anthem that had topped the UK charts, released a vocal duet with Elton that had been recorded some while before. Taken from her 'Heart Over Mind' album,

'Flames Of Paradise' failed to arrest the chart slump of the woman who had recorded the best selling single by a female in UK chart history. 'Flames' peaked outside the UK Top 50, though it reached the relative respectability of the US Top 40.

In America, Elton and Bernie were reunited at the fourth annual MTV Music Video Awards to receive a Special Recognition trophy. Geffen Records, with whom Elton had not re-signed for the US, preferring to return to MCA, saw fit to compile a 'Greatest Hits Volume Three, 1979–1987' album, but the law of diminishing returns had set in even further than they could have imagined. The US-only release performed little better chart-wise than 'Leather Jackets' (near the basement of the Top 100 of the *Billboard* chart), though it was certified platinum.

'Greatest Hits Volume Three' was also competing with the first album under the new MCA deal, 'Live In Australia', the double album/box set recorded during his 1986 tour, with the massive backing of the Melbourne Symphony Orchestra. The latter was finally released in the autumn of 1987; in Britain, it carried the personalised catalogue number EJBXL1. It was certified gold and stayed in the *Billboard* chart for over nine months, reaching the US Top 30; illogically, the platinum 'G.H. Vol.3' didn't make the Top 75 and charted for less than six months. Of the 14 tracks on the live album, no fewer than 11 were from the DJM years. This was a refreshing 'blast from the past' for Elton's loyal fans, as it was for Elton himself: 'When we started rehearsals in Brisbane,' he told the audience, 'I had to learn some of the words myself because these were songs I hadn't played for over a decade. And it made me realise how wonderful some of these words by Taupin are.' To make his point, he singled out 'The Greatest Discovery' from 1970's 'Elton John', one of six tracks selected from his breakthrough album, while both the title track and 'Tiny Dancer' were resurrected from the 'Madman Across The Water' LP. The three relatively new tracks were scarcely recent releases either: 'Tonight' dated from 1976's 'Blue Moves', as did 'Sorry Seems To Be The Hardest Word', while the final pick, 'Don't Let The Sun Go Down On Me', came from 'Caribou' (1974).

Of the DJM material, apart from the eight songs already mentioned, 'Burn Down The Mission' came from 'Tumbleweed Connection' and, finally, Elton's two best sellers from 1973, 'Don't Shoot Me, I'm Only The Piano Player' and 'Goodbye Yellow Brick Road', were raided for 'Have Mercy On The Criminal' as well as 'Candle In The Wind' (which made the Top 5 in the UK singles chart). All in all, the live album may not have broken any new ground but it probably introduced many of his younger fans to some back pages of which they may have been unaware, while simultaneously keeping older followers happy. And, despite those throat problems, he sounded as if he was enjoying himself.

All seemed to have ended well on the newsprint front until a certain press baron came sniffing round the Vicarage Road ground at Watford. Elton's love affair with Watford FC had been on the wane for a while and, while he would never lose his interest in the club, he had tired of 'having to tour when I didn't really want to, to buy a centre forward. If you want

to be chairman of a football club, you have to do that'. In actual fact, the rot had set in a few years earlier when the first of a number of managerial changes had seen Graham Taylor depart for Aston Villa, and ultimately the job of England teammanager. 'When Graham left,' Elton was to admit later, 'it didn't really have the same appeal.'

Front runner to purchase his controlling interest in Watford Football Club was the newspaper tycoon Robert Maxwell, the man whose *Daily Mirror* had been Elton's staunch defender in the tabloid mud-slinging. Understandably well disposed towards Maxwell, Elton wanted to assure a secure future for the club he loved, but the proposed takeover was halted in December when the Football League would not allow Maxwell to hold an interest in more than one club.

When the Football League's decision was revealed (but before it became clear that Maxwell was indeed a scoundrel), Elton was at pains to insist that he was not simply trying to sell the football team to the first person who could afford to purchase his shares, but felt that passing control to Maxwell would provide the club with the financial muscle to maintain its newly acquired status as a major force in English football. As he remarked, without a fresh injection of capital, 'we're back in the situation where if anything happens to me...'. He admitted that Maxwell was 'abrasive', but like the rest of the world (and particularly those who had relied on the pillaged pension fund), was taken in by Maxwell, with whom he said 'I got on well'. Elton's apparent desire to distance himself from his past was underlined when it was announced that Rocket Records

would effectively only continue as a label for Elton's own releases.

On January 28th, 1988, Elton inducted The Beach Boys into the Rock'n'Roll Hall Of Fame in New York. It wouldn't be the only time the veteran group and their avid supporter would get together that year. In June, Elton appeared at the sixth annual Prince's Trust Rock Gala at London's Royal Albert Hall, at the same time as 'I Don't Wanna Go On With You Like That' reached the UK Top 30. The single was far more successful in America,

where it became his first Top 3 hit (apart from the chart-topping Aids charity single, on which he shared the spotlight) since 'Little Jeannie' in 1980. It was the first single from his next album, 'Reg Strikes Back'.

If his apparent desire to be free of his commitments at Watford had seemed to hint at a new restlessness, the album, from its cover to its contents, seemed to confirm it. The sleeve was packed with onstage regalia, uniforms, glasses, and memorabilia, with Reg Dwight stepping out from behind them. He

The ELTON JOHN Collection

SOTHEBY'S
FOUNDED 1744

Above
A selection of Elton's Gold Discs
on view before the Sotheby's
auction

Right
Modelling some of the diamond
studed jewellery also auctioned

Left
The auction room at Sotheby's

Right
Elton's shoes on view at the auction

was obviously trying to distance himself from his professional alter ego that he had had to live with for many years, that of Elton John the superstar, and gradually found that going home to a residence which had effectively become nothing more than a giant trophy case was a distraction, to say the least.

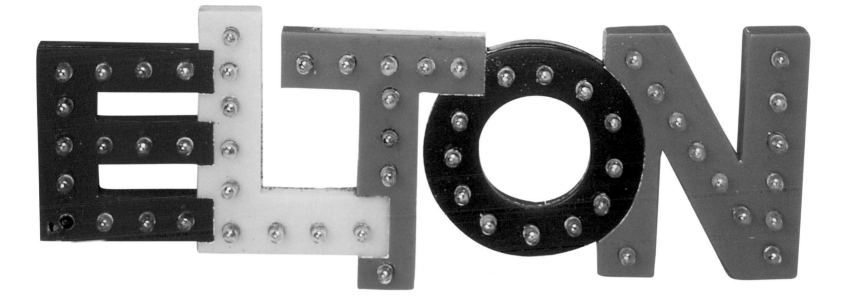

In early September 1988, 2,000 items of his memorabilia went under the hammer at Sotheby's auction house in London. Everything from gold discs to spectacles to his giant 'Pinball Wizard' boots (as worn in the *Tommy* film), which alone fetched $11,000, was on offer. Elton's habit of hoarding every item, and never disposing of anything, had resulted in what amounted to a fantastic museum of memorabilia which he felt was also true of his life, and he reasoned that a gigantic spring clean, a clearing out, was the best way to resolve his apparent feelings of confusion about his own identity.

Above
The famous 'Elton' spectacles

Right
The boots worn by Elton in the *Tommy* movie

Reg Strikes Back

The album, like 'Captain Fantastic' before
it, seemed to indicate a process of reappraisal
and, once again, renewed success followed
when it reached the Top 20 in both Britain and
America. It was surprising that the opening
track, 'Town Of Plenty', which featured Pete
Townshend of The Who on guitar, was only a
very minor UK hit single but, in the US, 'A
Word In Spanish' continued the revival in
Elton's fortunes by reaching the Top 20 of the
Billboard chart, his third single to reach such
heights in less than a year. Gus Dudgeon had
now been supplanted by Chris Thomas as
producer, leading to what some might feel was
a less ornate, more 'contemporary' sound, but
'Mona Lisas And Mad Hatters (Part 2)' bore
very little musical relation to the delicate
'Honky Chateau' track that had supposedly
inspired it, though it boasted an unusual guest
star in jazz trumpeter Freddie Hubbard.
Elsewhere it was the familiar crew of
Johnstone, Morgan, Paton, and Mandel,
although Nigel Olsson and Dee Murray
dropped by to make a familiar contribution to
the vocal harmonics, while percussionist Ray
Cooper played on four tracks.

Anyone reading the lyric book of 'Reg'
might have been somewhat disappointed with
the settings in which some of the songs had
been put. 'Goodbye Marlon Brando' had
potential on paper but was almost turned into
hookless heavy metal, while 'The Camera
Never Lies' and 'Heavy Traffic' were less than
memorable. The majority of the album was as
joyless as you might expect given the events
of the recent past. Elton was to subsequently
admit that 'Reg Strikes Back' was in some
ways therapy for him after a harrowing period

Left
During the Reg Strikes Back
tour, 1988

Right
Filming of 'A Word In Spanish' in
America, 1988

Sacrifice

which had seen his marriage end, his throat require emergency surgery and his career begin to falter after a strong renaissance in the early 1980s. It forced him to concentrate on something other than his problems, but, not surprisingly in view of his state of mind, included both good material and songs he admitted 'I didn't really like'.

By far the jolliest, most melodic track on offer was the closing 'Since God Invented Girls', a track which gave Beach Boys Bruce Johnston and Carl Wilson the chance to repay Elton for his kind words in January by pastiching themselves. 'I Don't Want To Go On With You Like That' just failed to top the US chart in September 1988 and, with supreme irony, the man blocking its ascent to become Elton's first solo US Number One since 1975's 'Island Girl' was George Michael with his 'Monkey'. Elton concluded a busy month even by his standards when he played five sell-out nights at New York's Madison Square Garden, beating the existing record for selling out The Garden previously held by The Grateful Dead. The support act was Wet Wet Wet, a young group of Scottish hopefuls who would emulate George Michael, the past beneficiary of Elton's musical patronage, and top the charts.

The musicians playing the Madison Square Garden dates would accompany Elton round the world: Davey Johnstone (guitar), Guy Babylon and Fred Mandel (keyboards), Romeo J Williams (bass) and Jonathan Moffett (drums), plus a trio of backing singers: Natalie

Jackson, Marlena Jeter and Mortonette Jenkins. While in America, Elton wrote and produced a minor hit single, 'The Rumour', for Olivia Newton-John, which charted just before his own third single from 'Reg Strikes Back', 'A Word In Spanish', reached the US Top 20.

November finally saw the announcement that Elton and Renate were set to divorce, albeit amicably, yet he remained wedded to Watford FC, if not totally by choice.

At the start of the 1988/89 season, he claimed (and few would have doubted it) that he had invested £3 million in the club and that buying a new player would probably involve him earning £1 million, but he also appeared to have regained his enthusiasm for Watford by reverting to frequent contact with the everyday events surrounding it. Sadly, it was not to prove a classic campaign for Watford, who had been relegated from the First Division the previous season. They would finish fourth, failing to bounce back to reclaim a place in the elite, and would flop to 15th the following term. In 1990, Elton finally found a suitable buyer in Jack Petchey, though he would retain the title of life president.

December 1988 saw a happy end to Elton's tabloid troubles with the *Sun*, the paper settling his libel suit out of court for £1 million plus a grovelling front-page apology. The Sun were 'delighted' they and Elton had 'become friends again, and are sorry that we were lied to by a teenager living in a world of fantasy'. At the end of the day, the singer revealed, his willingness to settle was inspired by the example of Ulsterman Gordon Wilson, whose dignity in the face of personal loss had recently been highlighted in the media. Wilson

had survived a terrorist bomb attack in which his daughter died as they lay buried together under debris, and Elton was seemingly so moved by his great courage and unselfishness that he was able to finally put his dispute with the *Sun* into perspective as comparatively unimportant compared with a father watching helplessly as his child died violently. By all accounts, it spurred Elton to 'shut up and get back to work'.

The stage was clearly set for a possible artistic renaissance.

After his dissatisfaction with 'Reg Strikes Back', Elton was determined the next album, his last of the 1980s, would be a milestone even by his own standards. For his part, Taupin spent a lot of time in England hanging out with his writing partner, and Elton would show his appreciation for Taupin's considerable contributions by dedicating the finished album to him as a token of how greatly he valued their continuing relationship and how much he was admired and respected by Elton. This was apparently because he had asked Taupin to create a theme which would permeate the album: 'we just wanted every song on it to be great'. According to Taupin, they had discovered a fresh common goal in the songs they had written resulting from discussions about their strengths, and Elton was allowing Bernie musical, as well as lyrical, input, which Taupin confirmed 'meant a great deal to me'. After the workmanlike but uninspiring 'Reg Strikes Back', an album which was little more than a colourful macedoine, the idea was to take inspiration from songs which they remembered as 'R&B classics' or favourite records from their formative years. This theme, ironically enough, was a similar homage to musical roots as that which Billy Joel (the piano playing singer/songwriter who had often been compared to Elton) pursued to multi-platinum effect with his 1983 album, 'An Innocent Man'. Taupin would tell Elton the inspiration behind his lyric, be it Ray Charles, Ben E King, Sam & Dave or whoever, and let the tunesmith do the rest. The man whose first record purchases were Jackie Wilson's 'Reet Petite' (ironically a UK chart-topper in 1986, almost three decades after it was originally released) and the Danny & The Juniors anthem, 'At The Hop', needed no second bidding. This heritage was something Eric Clapton had long been aware of: 'Elton's music always seemed to come from that R&B root,' the guitar star later suggested. 'His left hand would set up the groove, and Bernie's lyrics would give him the emotional angle that made the rest of the music grow.'

The integration of the songwriting process seemed to have the effect of speeding it up: the creation of the title track's melody, for instance, had begun one afternoon at 4.15pm with John seeing Taupin's lyrics for the first time: by 6.30pm, a finished composition and recording had been nailed. Location for the sessions was Puk Studios in Denmark, and, recording complete, March 20th saw Elton in Lyons, France, playing the first show of a 50-date European trek, with the familiar figure of Nik Kershaw his support act. Kershaw was at the time in need of a boost, his last Top 30 hit having come as long ago as December 1985: he would later become one of pop's backroom boys, writing hits for Jason Donovan and others.

Elton celebrated his 42nd birthday with a lavish £200,000 party in Paris, having caused palpitations a few days earlier by collapsing during a show in Paris where he had been performing an energetic dance routine. 'Apparently his blood pressure suddenly dropped,' said a production assistant. 'It was terribly hot.' But the show went on in time-honoured tradition. There were to be further celebrations in May, when he was invited to perform at the Songwriters Hall Of Fame 20th anniversary dinner at New York's Radio City Music Hall. To make his trip worthwhile, he was accorded the National Academy Of Popular Music's Hitmaker Award.

The end of that month saw the sold-out UK leg of the tour, while a duet with Aretha Franklin entitled 'Through The Storm' that coincided with the homecoming made the US Top 20 and the UK Top 50. Recording the track was not, it appeared, an experience Elton would remember with particular gratitude, because it transpired that although the track was a duet, Aretha and Elton did not record together at the time, and in fact only met after the event, which was probably when Elton revealed to 'Lady Soul' that the backing track had not been recorded in what he felt was the really correct key for his voice; as he said, 'I had to go for it'. On a happier note, he also contributed a rock'n'roll medley of Fats Domino's 'I'm Ready' and a touch of Elvis Presley's 'Let's Have A Party' to the Richard Perry-produced 'Rock, Rhythm & Blues' set which was released that year.

His six Wembley Arena nights that same month introduced his home-based fans to a new look, while the grand piano of former

In Eiffel Tower headgear, Paris, 1987

Left
Elton on stage at the Univerasl
Amphitheatre in Los Angeles
performing Pinball Wizard with
The Who, 1989

days had been supplanted by a digital keyboard – not so easy to rest your foot on while
rippling through the arpeggios. 'It's not a
£300,000 electric organ as you may have
read,' he explained, adding: 'Besides I thought
my organ was worth a million quid!' It wasn't
the last reference to the *Sun* saga. 'Thank you
for all your support over the last two years: I
couldn't have come through it without you'
raised a thunderous cheer. The set list gave a
good airing to early songs like 'Burn Down
The Mission' as well as mid-period hits like
'Philadelphia Freedom' and 'Daniel'. The forth-
coming album, 'Sleeping With The Past', had
not yet displaced its older predecessors.
Finally the encore, 'Saturday Night's Alright
For Fighting', performed in a lime green suit,
top hat and Lennon-style glasses, was
remarkably restrained.

'Constant, reliable, an unchanging icon of
British pop,' said the *Independent*. The UK
tour ended in early June, but brought little
respite in what was to prove a hectic year. The
day after the final show, Elton took part in 'Our
Common Future', a five-hour ecological-
awareness world telecast concert. His
American and Canadian tours would see him
visit over 50 cities while, during August, he
took the opportunity to recreate his role as the
Pinball Wizard at a benefit performance of
Tommy at the Universal Amphitheatre in Los
Angeles, starring alongside not only The Who,
but Steve Winwood, Patti LaBelle, Phil Collins
and Billy Idol.

While his live prowess had never been in
doubt, Elton knew he needed to end the
1980s on a high note as far as recording was
concerned, a challenge he accomplished with

'Sleeping With The Past', described by Elton as 'the first thing I've done for years without personal problems clouding my mind'. With similar reference points to 'Don't Shoot Me', it was an R&B-flavoured album, with a nod to Sixties soul. The omens were right for a best-seller, though reviews were scarcely ecstatic: 'Now better known in this country for his foot-ball team, his court cases and his souvenirs than for his pop music,' wrote *Q* magazine, '"Sleeping With The Past" probably won't do much to change that situation.' It would take much more, their reviewer gloomily concluded, 'to remind people in the UK that he's in fact a pop star and not merely a slightly eccentric national institution'. The first single from the album, 'Healing Hands', did little in chart terms to improve matters, only reaching the British Top 50.

Released in September, 'Sleeping With The Past' initially reached the UK Top 10 and the US Top 30. The band that backed Elton was essentially the Williams-Moffett-Johnstone-Mandel-Babylon outfit, with singers Jackson, Jeter and Jenkins providing suitably gospel-tinged backing. Vince Denham's sax playing added the final touch to the Drifters-influenced 'Club At The End Of The Street', with its 'Under The Boardwalk'-like harmonies. Chris Thomas was producing for the second successive album and, apart from the political slant on the opening 'Durban Deep', the story of a suffering South African miner, everything seemed geared to entertainment pure and simple. The quasi-spiritual 'I Never Knew Her Name' had a swagger which was reminiscent of 'I Guess That's Why They Call It The Blues', but many of the tracks on the album simply

stood on their own merit, as part of a coherent whole. The jewel in the crown was the ballad 'Sacrifice', but that song's moment of glory had yet to arrive.

It had long been a source of wonder that Elton, with millions of record sales to his name, had never enjoyed a solo British Number One single in his own right. Fourteen years after 'Don't Go Breaking My Heart', his duet with Kiki Dee, he finally made it with 'Sacrifice', almost inevitably a John/Taupin ballad. Apparently his 66th single release, it had been reissued (as a double A-side with the similarly revived 'Healing Hands') after some absolutely saturation airplay. 'Sacrifice' had been released in the United States first of all, where it reached the Top 20, but had peaked outside the UK Top 50 and was in the British chart for less than a month. In the early summer of 1990, after it had been decided that the single had been unjustly ignored, it was reissued after BBC Radio One's star disc jockey of the time, Steve Wright, had aired it every day, which meant that it was receiving the kind of mass listener exposure which could not be bought at any price. Elton was of course pleased, but decided that it would only be reasonable if he donated his royalties from the reissue to charity. It was a huge hit which remained at Number One in the British chart longer than any other single that year, and Elton was particularly delighted that its success also resulted in the 'Sleeping With The Past' album finally reaching the Number One position in the UK chart as well, over nine months after it had first been released, as he considered it 'one of the best albums I've done for a long time'.

Healing *Hands*

Sleeping With The Past

But it was the fact of 'Sacrifice' becoming his very first chart-topping solo single in Britain that excited him more. He reflected that his success in the first half of the 1970s had been very exciting, but that a combination of his own problems and an understandably blase attitude after so many world-beating achievements had diluted his enjoyment of it, but that he had adopted a different attitude to his life and his behaviour, and the success of the single had made him feel as excited as when he had achieved his very first hit: 'It was so exciting and it was an incredibly happy time for me'.

Elton used an appearance on a TV chat show to announce that the royalties from this and all his future singles would go to various Aids charities, while its success helped 'Sleeping With The Past' to sales of several million and, in July 1990, nine months after it was first released, it topped the UK album chart for five weeks. The decision to align himself with Aids research with 'Sacrifice' was taken after he had struck up a friendship with teenage haemophiliac Ryan White. When the boy finally succumbed to the disease, contracted after a blood transfusion, Elton sang 'Skyline Pigeon' and acted as pall bearer at the funeral in a church in Indianapolis. Four days earlier, on April 7th, he had made a surprise appearance at 'Farm Aid IV' in the Hoosier Dome, Indianapolis, dedicating 'Candle In The Wind' to Ryan who died just a matter of hours later.

The whole episode clearly affected the singer deeply. He vowed to donate all the royalties from any further singles he would be releasing – and he made it clear that he had

no intention of curtailing his recorded output, and expected to be making records and indeed singles for the foreseeable future – to Aids research. He considered that he could afford such generosity and preferred to make his donation in the form of record royalties rather than by playing benefit concerts, and noted that he had been more affected by the spread of Aids than by anything else. This was a major gesture which ultimately may prove to have been a considerable factor in helping to stamp out one of the most terrifying diseases to afflict the human race in the second half of the 20th century.

However, there was something closer to home to worry about. Following years of abuse, a close friend urged Elton to seek help and avoid possible self-destruction. Six weeks of 'recovery' in a Chicago rehabilitation clinic followed, to cure bulimia and addiction to drink and drugs.

A year off from recording and touring would follow. To plug the gap, a collections of past glories was released in the autumn of 1990. 'The Very Best Of Elton John' swept all before it in that year's Christmas album sales stakes, reaching Number One in Britain, although it was not released in the States. Despite the title, it was marked that the fertile if less commercially successful period between 'Your Song' and 'Rocket Man' had been omitted completely. In the US, a 4xCD boxed set titled 'To Be Continued . . .', which included hits, rarities (one of the Bluesology singles, 'Come Back Baby'; a live version of 'I Feel Like A Bullet (In The Gun Of Robert Ford)'; a duet with France Gall, a famous French chanteuse, on 'Donner Pour Donner', sung in French, etc.) and four brand new tracks produced by the extremely successful Don Was as well as a 40-page booklet made 'To Be Continued . . .' a very desirable item. It failed to equal the chart-topping feat of the British 'Very Best Of' double CD, but spent three months in the *Billboard* Top 200 albums chart, and was certified gold.

To follow the success of 'Sacrifice', 'You Gotta Love Someone', one of the tracks produced by Don Was which appeared on the boxed set (and which had also been featured on the soundtrack to the movie Days Of Thunder, which starred Tom Cruise and Nicole Kidman) was released as a single and reached the UK Top 40 and US Top 50. The boxed set belatedly appeared in Britain just before Christmas 1990, and another of the Don Was-produced tracks, 'Easier To Walk Away', was excerpted from 'To Be Continued . . .' and became a minor UK hit. The year of 1990 ended with what can only be described as a soul-baring exercise. 'Reg On the Radio' was a two-part Christmas special in which Elton went head-to-head with BBC Radio 1 DJ Richard Skinner. What happened next is best described by Skinner himself.

'The interview came at a vital point in Elton's life. He'd had a pretty bad time at the end of the Eighties, with his marriage breaking up, a court case involving the *Sun* newspaper, and a drinking problem. When I spoke to him, he'd just sold off all his famous costumes and he was having his Windsor house completely redone. He seemed to be trying to shed a lot of his past. We met in a house he'd rented in Holland Park, decorated with a strange mix of genuine Monet paintings and Wurlitzer juke-

boxes. There was just him and a butler living there – he told me it was the first time he'd ever lived on his own. During the break, he got up and made the tea himself, something the "big star" Elton would never have done ten years before. The interview was about his whole career, and he was happy to talk about anything and everything. He seemed to want to evaluate everything he'd done. He was in a very philosophical mood, but also very funny, joking around at every opportunity.'

As Skinner suggests, the course of the interview ranged from the early, struggling years, through to the *Sun*, matrimony and his recent solo chart-topper. There were many memorable moments during the two hours, one of the most interesting being 'If you could go back and talk to Elton John in 1972, what advice would you give him?' Without hesitation, Elton explained that nothing came to mind, since he had achieved the feat of becoming 'the biggest artist in the world' and greatly enjoyed the process, despite his lack of experience, which had actually added to his pleasure. He felt lucky that he had been able to relish his fame, 'especially in the earlier years', and was extremely grateful that he had accepted that an eventual decline in his fortunes was inevitable. This realisation, it appeared, had enabled him to regard everything which had subsequently happened in a positive light – even Elton John had apparently accepted that he was only human, although his achievements thus far might be considered quite superhuman. Many loose ends had been tied up in 1990, many wrongs righted and record books rewritten, but the next five years would see little relaxation of the pressure.

Elton and Bernie Taupin, 1989

Don't Let The Sun *Go Down On Me*

Rocket *Man*

Two *Rooms*

The *One*

Candle *In The Wind*

Sweat It *Out*

Runaway *Train*

Understanding *Women*

The Last *Song*

When A Woman

Emily

Doesn't Want You

Whitewash *County*

The *North*

Rare *Masters*

Friends

Simple *Life*

Border *Song*

Born *To Loose*

Duets

Love *Letters*

True *Love*

Teardrops

I'm *Your Puppet*

High *Society*

Ain't Nothing Like

Go On *And On*

The Real Thing

Old *Friend*

If You *Were Me*

Shakey *Ground*

When I Think *About You*

Duets *For One*

The *Power*

A Woman's *Needs*

Hakuna *Matata*

The *Lion King*

Circle *Of Life*

I Just Can't Wait *To Be King*

Can You Feel *The Love Tonight*

Reg Dwight's *Piano Goes Pop*

Bel*ieve*

Pl*ease*

Made In *England*

1991

Made In
England

1995

Made In

Nineteen ninety-one was a quiet year by Elton's standards. The reasons would become clearer as time passed and he revealed more about his recent past and the drastic changes in his lifestyle that had resulted. Full-scale touring and prolonged recording sessions were, for now, off the agenda. On the face of it, though, he was still very much out and about. In February, his revived chart fortunes brought him the award of Best British Male Artist at the annual Brit Awards at London's Dominion Theatre, while the following month saw him at a Carnegie Hall benefit show in New York for the Rainforest Foundation, in which he shared the spotlight for the first time with Sting.

England

Above:
Elton with Madonna,
backstage at the Brit Awards

They performed 'Come Down In Time' from 'Tumbleweed Connection', the song which the erstwhile Police star would later choose as his contribution to the 'Two Rooms' tribute album. Sting revealed that he had been impressed by the song the first time he ever heard it, and had taught himself to play it on guitar and even performed it during his early scuffling years. He found it lyrically cryptic with 'evocative images' which everyone could interpret in their own way. When he recorded it (apparently with Elton on piano, credited as Nancy Treadlight for some reason, but with no other backing apart from his own double bass), the minimalist approach created an atmospheric jazzy sound.

Although he had been absent from the recording studios of late, one of Elton's past hits seemed reluctant to go away. Originally released in 1974, 'Don't Let The Sun Go Down On Me' had seemed to become Elton's theme tune for middle age. A remixed version of the track was released in February 1991, presumably to promote Elton's 'Very Best Of' double album, but perhaps more significantly because it had become part of George Michael's live set. In March 1991, Elton encountered Michael back-stage at a Wembley concert and there they decided to duet on the song. When Elton came onstage, the crowd went wild, a moment recreated for the video that accompanied its release at the end of the year as a single; although the video was 'faked', the recording supposedly came from that initial Wembley performance. 'The video for the single was actually shot over several days,' confirmed Michael Pagnotta, the former Wham! star's publicist. It was shot in Burbank, California, where George Michael had been rehearsing.

Ever willing to upstage one of his oldest friends and rivals, April 1st saw Elton sharing a stage again, this time at Wembley Arena, where he gatecrashed long-time sparring partner Rod Stewart's concert, dressed to look like Stewart's new bride Rachel Hunter, to duet on 'You're In My Heart'. (To show there were no hard feelings, the new Mrs Stewart helped Elton with his make-up.) In May, he added his autograph to a piano that was being auctioned in Orlando, Florida, to raise money for the 'Give Kids The World' charity.

Meanwhile, the *Sunday Times* had published its annual list of rich Britons, in which Elton was rated at £100 million. With such riches behind him, he could clearly afford to take a year off, although his participation in a three mile walk to raise funds for Aids charities was a notable exception. 'From All Walks Of Life' took place in Atlanta, the city he now called his American home, having forsaken Los Angeles with few regrets, as he had clearly grown to dislike it, although perhaps not only due to the uninspiring music produced there, which he cited as one of the reasons for his disenchantment.

As the year drew to a close, Elton reviewed his career and personal life in a no-holds-barred conversation with David Frost on America's PBS (Public Broadcasting) TV channel. A number of revelations followed, including that between 1976 and 1990, his addiction to drugs and alcohol, his emotional swings and bouts of bulimia, had left him physically drained and out of condition.

Right
Elton pretends to be Rod Stewart's new bride. April Fools Day, Wembley Arena, London 1991

Far right
Duetting with George Michael

Don't Let The Sun
Go Down
On Me

Elton elaborated on his problems, telling Frost his mother had moved to Spain two years before with his stepfather, Fred, in protest at her son's excessive lifestyle, but had now returned to the UK.

He also paid tribute to Renate, whom it seemed he had not divorced as had been believed, though he had not remained in contact with her at her own request. He had apparently hoped that she could inspire him to reform, but realised that it was impossible to rebuild his approach to life in this manner, which led to his wife, who he called 'a wonderful girl', becoming completely unhappy.

From 1976 to 1990, Elton told Frost, he suffered from a great deal of extraordinary depression which led to uncharacteristic bouts of unpleasant and uncharitable behaviour and made him 'emotionally dead'. He went so far as to compare himself to Elvis Presley in his declining final years, but the catalyst was when he became aware that a person with whom he had fallen in love was trying to convince him that he needed immediate help, and that if he continued to refuse it, he was certain to die before long. Elton's response had been to check into a Chicago hospital where he was treated for alcoholism, cocaine addiction, bulimia and compulsive over-eating. On his discharge six weeks later, he'd given up alcohol, drugs, white flour and sugar and, equally important, rediscovered his self-esteem.

Elton freely admitted that he had been responsible for some deeds that he knew had been foolish and which he sincerely regretted. But he confessed that excessive consumption of both drugs and alcohol, which at first had appeared to be beneficial, ultimately led him to deep depression and a sense of helplessness, and this in its turn had prevented him enjoying his exotic lifestyle. He appreciated that it had been entirely his own fault, and was happy to have survived in good health. A three year period had been necessary before he was able to return to comparative normality, because he had been exhausted both physically and mentally, and his creativity had diminished. He felt that he had possibly released too many records and had performed live too frequently, and that a holiday away from his career would enable him to totally recover and to appreciate aspects of life which he had overlooked or dismissed. After his rehabilitation, he had decided to live on his own for the first time, in a house in West London, where his only companion was his dog, Thomas, whom he had adopted from the Battersea Dogs Home.

As he made his frank confessions to Frost, his duet with George Michael on 'Don't Let The Sun Go Down On Me' was being released as a single. While it provided Elton with his third British Number One – one solo, two shared – few of the thousands that bought it could have realised that Elton had advised Michael not to release it. Elton left a message for Michael reminding him that as the latter's 'Listen Without Prejudice' album had been less successful in the US than his previous multi-platinum 'Faith', it might be a mistake to release a live single at that point, although he agreed that it was an excellent record. Michael reassured him, and was proved correct when the single topped charts around the world. In February 1992, the track would be another US chart-topper for both artists.

While the Elton John/George Michael team had achieved major international success, it was the creative combination of Elton and Bernie Taupin that was held in highest regard by the industry. With innumerable tribute albums among the year's releases, it was no surprise when a collection of Elton & Bernie's compositions entitled 'Two Rooms' (after the '21 At 33' track 'Two Rooms At The End Of The World') was released in late 1991. According to Taupin, the title came from the one song he felt summed up his relationship with Elton. He explained that its message was a declaration that as individuals, they were prepared to accept that they were sometimes imprudent, but that those who criticised their work together should mind their own business. What made this particular tribute different from the rest was the high profile of the artists and the advertising campaign employed to sell both the album and a luxurious (and revealing) accompanying book.

Household names like Eric Clapton, Kate Bush, Sting, The Who, Rod Stewart and inevitably George Michael had all combined on the star-studded effort – something that Taupin clearly found thrilling. He was overcome with gratitude because so many famous artists whom he had idolised as a young unknown, and even earlier before he had decided to follow a career as a lyricist, had been keen to contribute to the 'Two Rooms' collection. Elton likewise echoed his partner's sentiments, reflecting that he was immensely proud that both he and Bernie were respected in this way by their rock music contemporaries, many of whom were 'good friends and great musicians'.

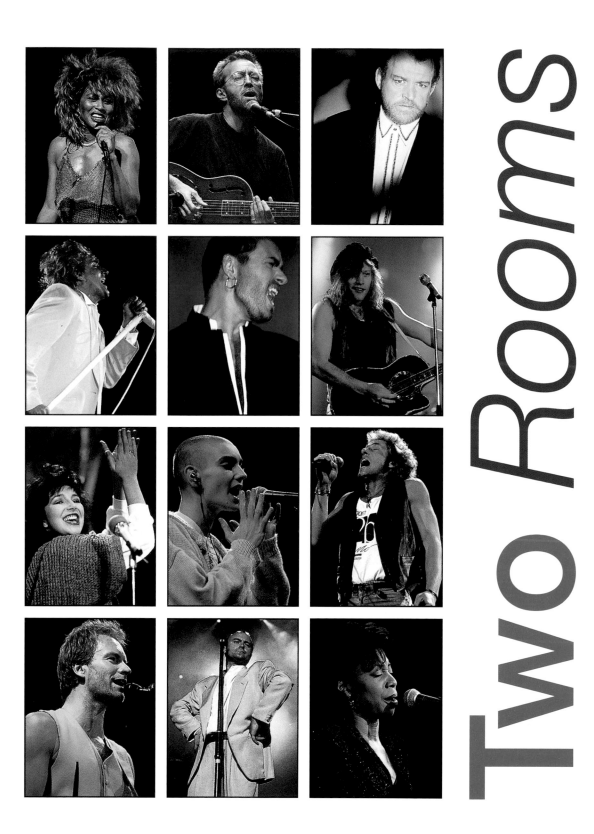

Two *Rooms*

That cast of friends included Oleta Adams ('Don't Let The Sun Go Down On Me'), The Beach Boys ('Crocodile Rock'), Jon Bon Jovi ('Levon'), Eric Clapton ('Border Song'), Joe Cocker ('Sorry Seems To Be The Hardest Word'), Phil Collins ('Burn Down The Mission'), Daryl Hall & John Oates ('Philadelphia Freedom'), Bruce Hornsby ('Madman Across The Water'), George Michael ('Tonight'), Sinead O'Connor ('Sacrifice'), Rod Stewart ('Your Song'), Tina Turner ('The Bitch Is Back') and Wilson Phillips ('Daniel').

A nationally networked TV show in late 1991 had given a fly on the wall view of the making of the album, together with tributes from those involved. The Who had contributed their version of 'Saturday Night's Alright For Fighting', which the group's charismatic singer, Roger Daltrey, regarded as one of Elton and Bernie's relatively few songs which were rockers as opposed to ballads, and he found it surprising that their output included such a small percentage of uptempo items. Daltrey and his bass-playing colleague, John Entwistle, recalled meeting Elton in the Sixties when they played in Watford, when he was Reg Dwight, and was upset because he had not been allowed to sing. This was, one would presume, when he was a member of Bluesology, at a time when that group also included Long John Baldry, Stuart Brown and maybe even Marsha Hunt. Singer Kate Bush's contribution to the 'Two Rooms' project – a reggae-tinged version of 'Rocket Man' – was particularly newsworthy, as she was enjoying one of her characteristic breaks from actual recording activity. However, she found this opportunity irresistible, especially as she was

given carte blanche to select the song she would record, which she likened at the time to the fulfilment of a dream.

Released on November 25th, 1991, and backed by a cover of 'Candle In The Wind' otherwise unavailable to the public, her single almost reached the UK Top 10. The album made Number One in Britain, and achieved platinum status in the US, where it reached the Top 20. Since Bernie Taupin had been called centre stage to share the spotlight, many people were given cause to wonder exactly where he'd hidden himself. The answer was simple. He was now living quietly in Los Angeles, in the same house he'd bought back in 1972. A long-time US citizen, he'd even flown his parents out to join him and his second wife, Toni.

It was a move that had surprised his writing partner, to say the least. Elton rightfully maintained that it would have been far more likely that of the two of them, he, with his many contacts with Hollywood and his natural flamboyance, would have relocated to North America, rather than the rurally-rooted Taupin, but regarded it as another example of the unpredictable nature of their partnership, also noting that while he himself preferred to stay in Britain, Taupin preferred to live in Los Angeles. There had also been a third Taupin solo album, 'Tribe', released in 1987 (a second Taupin album, 'He Who Rides The Tiger', on which Elton had appeared as a guest vocalist had appeared in 1980). Otherwise, he had been dabbling in rock video direction and – no mean feat, this – co-writing two US Number One singles: 'We Built This City' for (Jefferson) Starship and 'These Dreams' for Heart, both of

Left
Artists who recorded tracks on the 'Two Rooms' LP :

(first row)
Tina Turner - *The Bitch Is Back*

Eric Clapton - *Border Song*

Joe Cocker - *Sorry Seems To Be The Hardest Word*
(second row)
Rod Stewart - *Your Song*

George Michael - *Tonight*

Jon Bon Jovi - *Levon*
(third row)
Kate Bush - *Rocket Man*

Sinead O'Connor - *Sacrifice*

Roger Daltrey / The Who
- Saturday Night's Alright For Fighting
(bottom row)
Sting - *Come Down In Time*

Phil Collins - *Burn Down The Mission*

Oleta Adams - *Don't Let The Sun Go Down On Me*

which were collaborations with fellow British ex-patriate Martin Page.

Another name was to be added to the tragic list of Aids victims when Queen singer Freddie Mercury died in November 1991. Elton's floral tribute of 100 pink roses bore a card saying simply 'Thanks for being my friend: I will love you always'. This wasn't the only death Elton had had to deal with: bassist Dee Murray, who had settled in the States with his wife Maria, died on January 14th, 1992, of a massive stroke, following treatment for malignant melanoma. His widow gave Elton a photograph which was to prove an inspiration. It showed Elton and Murray during the latter's final tour as a member of Elton's band, and Elton felt that in the picture, he himself looked the way he remembered his father looking, except that Elton disturbingly looked older than his memory of his father ! He apparently kept the picture in a place where he would see it every morning, perhaps as a reminder to keep himself in good condition.

The following month saw him pick up a Grammy by proxy, as it were, when Irish flautist James Galway's version of 'Basque' won the Best Instrumental Composition award. In March 1992, Elton played two concerts at the Grand Ole Opry in Nashville to benefit the Dee Murray Family Memorial Fund. It was all a far cry from the Freddie Mercury Memorial Concert at Wembley Stadium in April 1992, when Elton's duet with Guns N'Roses star Axl Rose had brought the house down. Much was being made at the time of the Guns N'Roses, lead singer's undisguised anti-gay stance, as expressed in the song 'One In A Million'. But thanks, quite possibly, to Rose's

complimentary comments about Queen's music which had apparently made a tortured childhood more bearable, plus the fact that they were 1992's most bankable assets, the hatchets were buried. Even so, no one had expected Elton's personal seal of approval, in which he explained that he was no longer as youthful and energetic as had been the case in the past, and that he no longer regarded incorporating acrobatics into his stage act as an essential, whereas Rose, Elton went on, could provide the excitement that might otherwise be absent.

Elton reflected that before Rose took to the stage, he had heard a recording of Freddie Mercury singing 'Bohemian Rhapsody', which had made him feel very upset about the loss of his friend. He also made it clear that he was appearing at the Mercury tribute chiefly to honour the memory of the uniquely flamboyant vocalist rather than because Mercury had died of an Aids-related illness. He preferred not to mention that fact, lest it detracted from his sorrow at the sad and premature loss of a great star. He also mentioned that his thoughts had been with the surviving members of Queen, a group which had experienced its own internal problems, but had been prepared to bury the hatchet in memory of their late colleague. The emotional investment the show demanded clearly left Elton drained, and he was a notable absentee when the whole cast combined for a finale of 'We Are The Champions'. Elton preferred not to be involved in the backslapping finale which is often the climax to such concerts, because he felt so sad about the reason for it, and although he was pleased by the obvious

Left
With Axl Rose of Guns N'Roses on stage at the Freddie Mercury Memorial Concert, Wembley Stadium, April 1992

The One

enjoyment of the crowd, reflected that it would have been preferable if Mercury himself had been able to dominate the stage again.

The Freddie Mercury tribute concert at Wembley Stadium was also the first time Elton had appeared in public with his new hairstyle - when he was asked if comments such as one which suggested he was wearing a dead animal had upset him, he admitted to initial annoyance, but later had found the comment amusing. As he said, the important thing was that he was pleased with it himself, and he likened the subject of his hair to his admission of bisexuality, in that he had to be prepared for an element of controversy and amusement at his expense. But it was time for the laughing to stop. 'Sleeping With The Past' had proved both a critical and commercial hit, so the pressure had been on to deliver when Elton and his entourage had entered the Guillaume Tell studios in Paris in November 1991 for five solid months of hard work, give and take the interuption of seasonal festivites.

With its elaborate Versace-inspired artwork, 'The One' was released in June 1992, days after Elton kicked off his first world tour for three years. He'd taken a leaf out of football sponsorship and had the tour underwritten by make-up manufacturers Revlon, a nod perhaps to the glam glitter and greasepaint he'd long been known for, but things would have a rather different style this time round. Italian haute couturier Gianni Versace followed his cover design through to clothe the eight-piece band and decorate the stage they played on. There was also a souvenir video instead of a conventional tour programme, while Elton, so often the reluctant showman, had clearly

rediscovered his appetite.   He remarked that he intended to enjoy himself, also admitting that he had made similar claims in the past, but had not been really been convinced that what he was saying was accurate. This time, he felt in better physical condition than for his previous tour, and had been playing tennis every morning with a professional. He was now spending his wealth on improving and maintaining his health rather than indulging hedonistic and often extreme indulgences.

His 31st UK chart album in 22 years (and his 32nd in the US, where 'The Thom Bell Sessions' counted as a mini-album with its three songs), 'The One' just failed to unseat Lionel Richie's 'Back To Front' from the top spot, and also, remarkably, became Elton's first US Top 10 album for 15 years, since 'Blue Moves'. Eric Clapton (with whom he had just played a series of high-profile, double-header concerts at Wembley Stadium) guested on guitar and shared lead vocals for 'Runaway Train', while 'The One' itself was a trademark ballad that could hardly fail as the lead single – and didn't. It reached both the US & UK Top 10, and would be followed two months later by 'Runaway Train', which almost reached the Top 30 on both sides of the Atlantic.

His rhythm section was an interesting choice: Olle Romo, a metronomic drummer known for his work with Eurythmics (another ex-Eurythmics band member, Jonice Jamison, was among the backing vocalists), and Pino Palladino, the Welsh/Italian master of the fretless bass, who had been the backbone of Paul Young's sound. While Elton contributed the keyboards to each track as usual, he was 'shadowed' by Guy Babylon, while Mark Taylor added a third keyboard on a several tracks. This, combined with credits for 'programming', led to a lush and very 'produced' sound, most notable on tracks like 'Sweat It Out' and 'Understanding Women', which married both electronic keyboards and percussion with Elton's familiar piano arpeggios. The latter track also featured a distinctive guitar solo from Pink Floyd's Dave Gilmour, although on the rest of the album the ever-faithful Davey Johnstone was in evidence.

Given his by now well-publicised sexual preferences, Elton's performance of 'Understanding Women' and, more tellingly, 'When A Woman Doesn't Want You', required a certain suspension of belief but, as ever, Elton was acting out the part Bernie Taupin had written, to his own musical soundtrack. Other tracks were equally downbeat, though perhaps less unlikely. 'The Last Song' was about a deathbed reconciliation of a father and his son, encompassing a conversation concerning subjects which had never been mentioned to ultimately arrive at a liberating agreement.Royalties from 'The Last Song' were donated to six different charities.

Musically, it opened with a cheeky steal from Paul McCartney's 'Yesterday'. Recording the demo had, Elton admits, reduced him to tears, coming as it did just after the death of Freddie Mercury, but there were other, more personal reasons, why the song so moved him: 'I never made peace with my own father before he died,' Elton revealed to Vox magazine, 'and part of that is my own fault. I just didn't want to. I didn't know whether I regretted it or not but it has led to a lot of friction between myself and his wife, which is sad. As

I get more and more sober [and] lead a more clean-living life, it's nice to try and close these chapters.' Little wonder that 'The Last Song', the last and by far the shortest song on the album at under three and a half minutes, featured in many critical plaudits: *Q* summed up the album as: 'One great song, a few deft touches and some stodge.' When released as a single, 'The Last Song' almost reached the Top 20 in both Britain and America.

'Emily' also dealt with death, but in a rather different way, as Elton explained it was not about the disturbing premonition felt about death, but about re-meeting relatives who had previously died. He added that he was fearful of dying because he had no idea what it might involve, and was uncertain about how he should prepare himself for such a final journey.

Elsewhere, Taupin waxed autobiographical in 'The North', insisting that though a steel cloud used to follow him around, he was by then free of its hold on him. This bleak, effective, sparse offering followed the jolly 'Tumbleweed Connection'-style hoedown of 'Whitewash County' and left little doubt as to where he preferred to be.

July 1992 found Elton in Spain's Barcelona Stadium, where his show was broadcast as part of BBC Radio One's 25th anniversary celebrations. The ninth annual MTV Awards in Los Angeles saw a Wembley replay – this time a guest appearance on piano with Guns N'Roses. Their 'November Rain' followed his own performance of 'The One', which by this time was well on its way to the US Top 10. If Elton had reason to prefer hits to writs after recent events, he would be disappointed twice over as the year ended.

In September, he was sued by Los Angeles songwriters George Saadi and Ray Pickens, who alleged he 'knowingly or sub-consciously' had based 'Whispers', an instrumental track on 'Sleeping With The Past', on the tune of their 'Only Memories', a cassette copy of which Saadi claimed he gave to Elton at a 1984 backstage meeting. The following month, Elton was himself obliged to turn to law after a syndicated TV show Hard Copy and Paramount Pictures Corporation allegedly invaded his privacy. He filed a lawsuit in an Atlanta court citing extortion, slander, invasion of privacy, etc. The show had apparently reported that he had moved to Atlanta to be near an Aids treatment centre, and a reporter had allegedly used a helicopter to spy on him at his home and threatened to run a negative story on the star if he declined to give him an interview.

During a run of six sell-out dates at Madison Square Garden, Elton became the first non-athlete to be inducted into the venue's Walk Of Fame. Having just appeared before a combined audience of over 100,000, he then returned to Madison Square Garden for an Elizabeth Taylor Aids Foundation benefit, sharing the stage with Bruce Hornsby, George Michael and Lionel Richie. Even more fans would witness him breaking the house record at the Azteca Stadium, Mexico City, when two crowds totalling 180,000 saw his show. He would subsequently cancel concerts in Brazil and Chile, citing tiredness, but still seemed

Above
Elton with his award for the venue's Walk Of Fame at Madison Square Garden, New York, 1992

Right
With Elizabeth Taylor (right) and Billie-Jean King (left) on the night of the Elizabeth Taylor Aids Foundation benefit, 1992

indefatigable wherever charity activity was concerned: having helped raise funds for Neil Young's special school, he went on to take part in the Los Angeles Aids Project's 'Commitment To Life' cocktail/dinner party and benefit honouring Barbra Streisand and David Geffen. Also near the end of 1992, Elton and Bernie Taupin signed a massive song publishing deal with Warner/ Chappell Music for the rights to their entire post-1974 back catalogue and future compositions. The deal was estimated at a record $39 million.

A chapter of Elton's sporting life came to an end in early 1993, when he resigned as a director of Watford FC. 'Over the last two years, Elton's constant touring and recording schedule has been particularly punishing,' Watford director (and long-time music business friend) Muff Winwood said. 'It will keep him away from the UK for the foreseeable future, but we know he will be on the phone regularly, as eager as ever for results and news.' Indeed, he remained a shareholder and honorary vice-president of the club. Reports that he was taking acting lessons in preparation for a starring role in a film about another songwriting legend, Cole Porter, failed to become reality, like so many other speculative stories. On a more certain note, 'Simple Life' became a US Top 30 hit, thus breaking Elvis Presley's record as the artist with the most consecutive years (23) in the *Billboard* Top 40 singles chart. In Britain, it peaked just outside the Top 40.

Elton and Aretha Franklin
rehearse their duet of 'Border
Song' 1993

Clearly more important than any screen
stardom, or indeed hit singles, was the Elton
John Aids Foundation, which was launched in
early 1993. During a speech in San Francisco,
accepting a $250,000 donation to the charity,
he explained his reasons for launching it; he
admitted that he had been fortunate to avoid
becoming HIV positive when he was at a low
ebb, but was delighted to be in the best of
health, and wished to repay fate for his good
luck. He wanted to make it clear that to be
alive was extremely important, and to convince anyone who doubted it of that fact. The
profits from all his singles now went towards
Aids research, as did the proceeds from his
European gigs in mid-1993.

In April, Aretha Franklin invited him onto a
TV special, taped at New York's Nederlander
Theatre, to benefit the Gay Men's Health
Crisis: they duetted on 'Border Song'. It had
been the best part of two decades since he'd
provided Billie Jean King and her Philadelphia
Freedom tennis team with their anthem.
September saw the new slimline Elton com-
bining with his great friend, the multiple
Wimbledon champion, to beat Martina
Navratilova and Bobby Riggs at a Los Angeles
tennis tournament.

The release in early 1993 of a double, 37-
song CD package entitled 'Rare Masters' had
achieved the unlikely aim of digitalising the
'Friends' soundtrack. 'A fair enough repackag-
ing ploy,' said *Q* magazine, but still only gave
the package two stars out of a possible five.
Elton completists, however, were delighted, as
'Rare Masters' collected B-sides, obscure 45s
and album out-takes and, though its scope
was limited to the DJM pre-1975 period, it

was undoubtedly successful in filling the holes in many a collection. Tracks included 'Rock Me When He's Gone', 'Screw You', 'Let Me Be Your Car' (written for Rod Stewart), plus Paul Buckmaster's first string arrangement for Elton, 'Bad Side Of The Moon'.

Elton's second and more significant release of the year would come in December, by coincidence within a month of a similarly titled album by Frank Sinatra. Recorded in just a couple of months at a number of different studios and under as many different producers, 'Duets' turned Elton's propensity to sing with anyone at the drop of a hat to his own advantage. The song selections and the pairings ranged from the predictable to the positively inspired. Firmly in the latter camp was the link with Leonard Cohen on 'Born To Lose'. The arrangement gave the veteran Canadian, whose career had been in full flower just as Elton had burst onto the early-1970s scene, every opportunity to shine. His parting, ad-libbed shot 'And now, Elton, I'm losing you' was, as more than one critic noted, a memorable flourish.

Elton's love of Sixties soul, dating back to Bluesology days, was very apparent in the choice of the James & Bobby Purify hit 'I'm Your Puppet' and Marvin Gaye/Tammi Terrell's 1968 classic 'Ain't Nothing Like The Real Thing': these were faithfully reproduced in the company of Paul Young and Marcella Detroit respectively. Detroit, lead singer with Shakespear's Sister, was previously known as Marcy Levy under which name she had worked with, among others, Eric Clapton in the 1970s, co-writing the million-selling 'Lay Down Sally'. An Eighties soul classic, Womack

Elton opening a new centre for the Landmark Trust Charity

& Womack's 'Teardrops', allied him with the fast-rising Canadian star k d lang, who first achieved international fame as a country artist modelling herself vocally and in other ways on the legendary Patsy Cline. The track was produced by lang's collaborator Greg Penny, of whom more later. Two more distaff duets were in prospect on Ketty Lester's much-covered 'Love Letters' (with recent Grammy-winner Bonnie Raitt, which was included on the 'Duets' album) and Cole Porter's 'True Love'. The latter reunited the tried and tested pairing of Elton and Kiki Dee, so it was no surprise when Narada Michael Walden's production was excerpted as the Christmas single, an update of the Bing Crosby and Grace Kelly version from the 1956 movie, *High Society*.

Hopes that it would follow Elton and Kiki's earlier collaboration to the top of the charts and supply the Christmas Number One were, however, dashed: 'True Love' reached the UK Top 3 but was unable to reach the top because the eponymous debut single by Mr Blobby, a gruesome piece of pink rubber with yellow spots created by TV show host Noel Edmonds, made Christmas 1993 musically unmemorable . . . and almost unbearable! Elton and Kiki Dee's 1976 chart-stormer was revisited on 'Duets' but his partner this time round was RuPaul, a tall American transvestite with whom he would co-host the 1994 BRIT Awards Show. The song was given a suitably retro treatment courtesy of the famed Eurodisco producer Giorgio Moroder but, as one of the album's less inspired tracks, was never going to hit the heights as a charting single, despite it featuring an amusing Sonny & Cher pastiche.

Duets

Nik Kershaw, Elton's ex-backing guitarist and touring partner, weighed in with a new song, appropriately titled 'Old Friend'. He played all the instruments, as did Stevie Wonder on 'Go On And On'. Easier on the ear by far were Chris Rea's easy-paced, undemanding 'If You Were Me' and soul-rap duo PM Dawn's 'When I Think About Love', the latter inspiring a lyrical piano solo from Elton, while ex-Eagles vocalist Don Henley turned in an impressively gruff rendition of the 1975 hit by The Temptations, 'Shakey Ground'. Two of the songs were John/Taupin originals: 'The Power' (duetted with Little Richard and co-produced by Elton and Greg Penney, with backing vocals from gospel stars The Andrae Crouch Singers) and 'A Woman's Needs', shared with country diva Tammy Wynette. The penultimate track offered the 'bonus' of 'Don't Let The Sun Go Down On Me', if by chance anyone interested hadn't bought it yet, while the closer, 'Duets For One', was co-written with Squeeze lyricist Chris Difford. At the end of the day, the major surprise was the absence of Rod Stewart.

Elton's perspective on the project was simple enough. 'I just chose a lot of people that would be nice to work with,' he told *Q*. When asked if there was anyone left he'd like to duet with, he pinpointed Michael Stipe, lead singer with American cult band turned stadium rockers REM, who emerged from the state of Georgia (Elton's home base in America), such a venture could not be ruled out for the future. 'Duets' was to some extent both a crowd-pleaser and a holding exercise, offering little new to satisfy the critics but supplying record buyers with the ideal Christmas stocking-filler.

No surprise then that the critics let loose a broadside. Q magazine highlighted 'a disappointing lack of spontaneity and indeed fun, about the whole exercise' concluding that the album represented 'a missed opportunity to be a little less self-referential and to let down his hair'. Max Bell in *Vox* highlighted the Aids royalties link before spoiling the effect somewhat: 'I'd pay them not to release showbiz mush like this which by annual coincidence is timed to fill in that black hole in the calendar when sanctimonious humbug is abroad.' Yet as the album's UK Top 5 success proved (rather more than its disappointing Top 30 peak in the *Billboard* album chart), Elton retained a groundswell of public support, affection and admiration that few, if any, of his surviving 1970s contemporaries could hope to rival. Despite the make-up and glamorous stagewear, he was clearly flesh and blood underneath; he recalled in 1989 that he had failed to remember the lyrics to 'Candle In The Wind', adding that had he been Rod Stewart, he would have encouraged the audience to sing them which could have allowed him to conceal his confusion, but that he had found his forgetfulness extremely upsetting. The only redeeming aspect of the entire episode in Elton's eyes was that it emphasised his ability to be less than perfect on occasion.

Perhaps it was that very fallibility which had been the secret of Elton John's two and a half decades of success.

Yet anyone who underestimated him did so at their own risk, as the *Daily Mirror* found to their cost when they were ordered to pay £350,000 in libel damages for printing a false story about Elton headlined 'World Exclusive:

Ray Cooper on stage at The Royal Albert Hall, London November 1994

Elton's Diet of Death'. In refuting the story, Elton told the High Court: 'As far as my career is concerned, the most satisfying thing I have done was to admit I had problems – and to start the recovery process. For this article to nonchalantly toss that away without substantiation is most disgraceful and extremely hurtful.' With Elton's continuing experience of the legal system, it must have been tempting to advise George Michael when he started an action against his record label Sony (formerly CBS) in 1992 which came to court two years later. Yet his main concern, he revealed to *Q*, was to provide friendly support. Elton was uncertain whether Michael had been prudent in taking the multi-national corporation to court, but emphasised that his erstwhile duet partner had personally decided to pursue what he believed to be natural justice, and was aware of the potential pitfalls. Elton simply wanted Michael to know that someone cared about his fate and what might happen if he was unsuccessful, and explained that the young superstar genuinely felt his was a just cause, and had an idea of what to expect if the judge disagreed.

Elton had taken steps back to the stage in the summer of 1994 in tandem with Billy Joel, the American keyboard playing singer/songwriter whom critics had claimed owed much to Elton's blueprint in his early days. Their 21-date US stadium tour in the summer sold out in record time, surpassing The Rolling Stones and Springsteen in some cases. Back home in November 1994, he linked with Ray Cooper for shows at London's Royal Albert Hall, including an Aids foundation night with George Michael guesting. The year

The *Lion King*

wasn't scheduled to see a new Elton John album but, nevertheless, it did see the release of two works to which he had made a major contribution, albeit two decades apart! The first was the soundtrack to the Walt Disney cartoon feature film *The Lion King*, which paired him once more with lyricist Tim Rice. Soundtrack specialist Hans Zimmer, whose credits included such noted films as *A World Apart* and *Rain Man*, supplied the incidental music with which the John-Rice compositions were interspersed.

The combination of Rice and John worked well, even if there was more than a touch of *Joseph* about the likes of 'I Just Can't Wait To Be King' and 'Hakuna Matata'. 'Can You See The Love Tonight' worked on its own merits as one of Elton's most endearing ballads, while African-style chants added charm and atmosphere to 'Circle Of Life'. The musicians used on the sessions included Chuck Sabo (drums), Phil Spalding (bass) and Davey Johnstone (guitar), plus two interesting backing vocalists: Rick Astley, a former UK chart-topper back in 1987 with 'Never Gonna Give You Up' but whose talents had been discarded by the teen generation, and his current counterpart, Gary Barlow of Take That. Elton had ventured favourable opinions about Barlow's songwriting, and it seemed he might be one to watch in the future should he, like George Michael before him, escape the teen trap that had snared Astley and graduate to 'serious' music.

Buoyed by the school holiday rush to the cinema, the album reached the UK Top 5 and spawned two Top 20 singles, 'Can You Feel The Love Tonight' and 'Circle Of Life'. These tracks, along with 'I Just Can't Wait To Be King', were included on the soundtrack album with Elton's own vocals, as well as in the form in which they had been heard in the film (with the animated characters singing). On 'I Just Can't Wait To Be King', these included comic actor Rowan Atkinson, while 'Be Prepared', one of two John/Rice songs along with 'Hakuna Matata', featured a very unusual combination of talents: British actor Jeremy Irons with US actress Whoopi Goldberg and Cheech Marin, now a comedy actor but once half of the marijuana-fixated comedy duo, Cheech and Chong.

In early 1995, the film would become America's biggest video release, selling an astounding 26 million copies in less than two weeks and grossing £300 million. To put this into perspective, Disney's two previous biggest sellers, *Snow White* and *Aladdin*, had only sold 24 million in total, and while no one, even Elton himself, would ascribe its success to their contribution, it had clearly helped.

If *The Lion King* had been a multi-million dollar venture which expected to recoup all that and more at the box office, the second 1994 album was something that was low budget by anyone's standards. The small RPM label, based in East London, had come up with the ingenious idea of collecting some of the tracks an impoverished Elton had recorded back in the early Seventies for the 'Top Of The Pops' series of albums featuring covers of contemporary hits. The result was an album called 'Reg Dwight's Piano Goes Pop', a release that eventually received Elton's official blessing, with the proviso that a donation should be made to charity in lieu of royalties.

Elton's hosting of the 1994 BRIT Awards with drag queen RuPaul had hardly been a highpoint of his career; happily, the 1995 Brits proved an altogether different proposition. The choice of Elton John for an outstanding achievement in music award, following in the footsteps of Rod Stewart (1993) and Van Morrison (1994), was hardly a closely guarded secret, but the man receiving the accolade in front of the assembled ranks of music biz movers'n'shakers seemed underwhelmed. In a TV interview earlier in the day, he had declared that 'They usually give you these kind of awards when you're decrepit,' which, combined with his onstage declaration, 'There's life in the old girl yet', suggested that he was obviously not considering retirement . . .

This was far from the end of the prize giving, as the 37th Grammy Awards ceremony in early March included Elton in an all-embracing recognition of traditional British pop and rock talent. Along with him on the winners rostrum stood three major talents: The Rolling Stones, who won best rock album and best short form video; Pink Floyd, who turned in the best rock instrumental performance; and, last but not least, Elton's old chum Eric Clapton, whose 'From The Cradle' was judged best traditional blues album.

For Elton's part, this was to be a double Grammy occasion: not only did he win best male vocal pop performance for 'Can You Feel The Love Tonight', but he shared *The Lion King* soundtrack's accolade for the best album for children. His five separate nominations had included two in the best song category for 'Can You Feel The Love Tonight' and 'Circle Of Life'. One final bout of backslapping remained:

Above
The Brit Awards, London 1995

Right
Elton receiving his award for outstanding achievement in music at the Brit Awards, 1995

Elton and Tim Rice holding their
''*Lion King*' Oscars, Hollywood,
California 1995

the Oscars, in which the John/Rice team had
all but monopolised the nominations. Three
different *Lion King* songs had been nominated,
leaving a first Oscar a mere formality – 'Can
You Feel The Love Tonight' was the song
selected. This acclaim coincided with the
release of a new Elton album in late March
1995. The title was to be 'Made In England',
which replaced 'Believe' at the last minute,
and even before its release it was being called
'his best record for many years'.

Each of the eleven tracks boasted Taupin
lyrics, while fresh production values had been
introduced by the engagement of Greg Penny,
best known for collaborating with k d lang on
her classic 'Ingenue' album and since that for
his work with Scots songstress Eddi Reader
(previously with 'Perfect' hitmakers Fairground
Attraction). It wasn't the first time Elton and
Greg had worked together however, having
been introduced at the sessions for 1993's
'Duets' in which lang had participated. In point
of fact, the producer and artist had apparently
first met many years before that, in 1973,
when, as a 16-year-old fan, Penny had visited
the studio when bass player Dee Murray was
laying down his part to 'Saturday Night's
Alright For Fighting'.

Bernie Taupin's involvement was more
than a words-by-mail affair, as John Reid was
to confirm to *Music Week* magazine. Taupin
had apparently remained in England throughout the entire recording of the album, which,
Reid suspected, was longer than any of his
visits in 'about 15 years'. He already had
ready-prepared lyrics to several songs, but
continued to write more during his lengthy
sojourn back in the United Kingdom.

Made In *England*

The album had actually been recorded during the first half of 1994, but release had been held back due to the ongoing success of Elton's film music. It would have been foolish to release the new album while *The Lion King* was gathering awards, acclaim and sales, and Reid claimed that the completed 'Made In England' album had been kept under his personal control for six months so that it would sound new to everyone involved.

The venue for the sessions had been Lyndhurst, Hampshire, where legendary Beatles producer George Martin had established his new Air Studios complex. Long-time confederate Paul Buckmaster put in an appearance to provide his trademark string arrangements, allowing George Martin to orchestrate one track, 'Latitude', his use of french horn harking back to Beatles days. Elton had already become acquainted with the Lyndhurst studios when recording a contribution to harmonica player Larry Adler's all-star 'The Glory Of Gershwin' project, again with George Martin in attendance.

The first single, 'Believe', was issued in advance of the album and garnered huge airplay, reaching the UK Top 20. Many of the song titles were one-word affairs. One that critics homed in on was 'Belfast' which, because of the time lapse between recording and release, had been written when 'The Troubles' were still in almost daily evidence. Now the song was being unleashed on a waiting world after several months of (relative) peace in the province, a change Elton was well aware of. He was very relieved that the song was so positive and looked for the silver lining in even dreadful circumstances.

The promotional campaign for the album, plus the follow-up single 'Please', was based around the title's theme. '"Made In England" refers to the fact that Elton was born here, has roots here and lives here,' said Mercury Records marketing director Jonathan Green. 'But it also stands for old traditions of quality and fine craftsmanship.' The scope of the LP's promotional campaign would be huge, Green promised, 'especially as Elton has made himself more available for promotion than for a very long time.' There would be 'at least four singles' from the album during 1995, with the title track a contender for release in that format. The song seems to make direct reference to its singer's sexuality in the line 'You can still say homo, And everybody laughs.' Elton went on to justify the use of this taboo term by reflecting that it was symptomatic of the way homosexuality was regarded in Britain, as amusingly odd. Elton no doubt had experience of being on the receiving end of such abuse, but had felt secure on the few occasions when it had occurred.

This excitement in the music business permeated into the public at large, and there could have been few potential buyers unaware of the album's imminent release. This was due in large part to a pair of high-profile interviews bestowed upon the British rock press; a cover story in *New Musical Express* (how long had it been since he was last hip enough to be accorded that honour?) and the monthly rock magazine, *Q*. Perhaps surprisingly, it was the latter that made more waves. Elton considered *Q* 'the only decent music magazine that I read, really; very fair, the only one of real quality'. He appeared on the cover clad in a bright pink

In fancy dress at his 47th birthday party.

suit and eating chips out of a crumpled copy of the *Sun*, the tabloid newspaper he had beaten in the courts a few years before. The basic theme of the calculatedly outrageous article was excess, notably the various drugs the star had consumed during some of the peak (and manic) periods of his spectacular success. 'I took cocaine every four minutes' the front cover headline claimed, while a memorable phrase inside suggested, 'Sometimes when I'm flying over the Alps, I think, "That's like all the cocaine I sniffed."'

Though his responsibility with Watford Football Club was now merely that of honorary president, he clearly remained devoted to the club. In late 1994, he renewed a three year lease on a box at Vicarage Road, asking that it be used to let underprivileged children enjoy the match in comfort when he could not attend himself and, as if further to underline his continued moral – if no longer financial – commitment to the club's cause, he took the time to provide soccer weekly *90 Minutes* with an in-depth two page interview in March 1995. Trailed on the cover under the banner 'Watford Saved My Life', he claimed 'The football club helped me through a really difficult time. It gave me something else to do, rather than be Elton John all the time.' That same month, the *Sun* held him in their relentless spotlight again. This time, though, it was merely to state that he was now only the second richest British rock star, his alleged annual earnings of £17.6 million having been overtaken by Phil Collins with £22.2 million.

The Elton John of the mid Nineties is indeed a vastly different creature to the rather diffident singer/songwriter who had tiptoed

out of the backrooms of Tin Pan Alley three decades previously – and not only in monetary terms. He represents both a household name and image to the extent that there have been at least two sound and lookalike acts: Elton Oliver, an Englishman, and Elton Jack, from Australia. The year would hold two more anniversaries for Elton: the first being his 30th year as a full-time rock musician (since Bluesology turned pro) and the second his 25th anniversary as a chart act. As 'Please' (from 'Made In England') was to aptly suggest, 'After everything we've been through, what's left to prove?' Even so, Elton made the very definite decision to take his new album to the world. An ambitious touring schedule for 1995 saw him in the United States in the spring, moving to Europe during the summer and taking in Great Britain later in the year. After a Yuletide break, and maybe a visit to watch Watford playing a game or two, the tour was scheduled to move to South America in the early months of 1996.

As ever, though, for Elton Hercules John the road led onward and upward. He still refused to think about anything other than the future, and was not interested in reliving even the triumphs of his past, although the rewards for doing so would inevitably be immense. He explained that he simply wanted to continue to compose music which would entertain and be appreciated by others, because 'that is a wonderful thing to do'. A final word to Sir Tim Rice, whose opinion of Elton was clearly expressed on a television chat show just after their joint Oscar triumph: 'He's one of the great composers of the whole century, I think.'

No argument!

Year	Title
1969	**Empty Sky**

Empty Sky/Val-Hala/Western Ford Gateway/Hymn 2000/Lady What's Tomorrow/ Sails/The Scaffold/ Skyline Pigeon/Gulliver; Hay Chewed; Reprise

| **1970** | **Elton John** |

Your Song/I Need You To Turn To/Take Me To The Pilot/No Shoe Strings On Louise/First Episode At Hienton/Sixty Years On/Border Song/The Greatest Discovery/The Cage/The King Must Die

| **1970** | **Tumbleweed Connection** |

Ballad Of A Well Known Gun/Come Down In Time/Country Comfort/Son Of Your Father/My Father's Gun/Where To Now St Peter/Love Song/Amoreena/Talking Old Soldiers/Burn Down The Mission

| **1971** | **17-11-70** |

Take Me To The Pilot/Honky Tonk Woman/Sixty Years On/Can I Put You On/Bad Side Of The Moon/Burn Down The Mission (including My Baby Left Me/Get Back)

| **1971** | **Friends (Soundtrack)** |

Friends/Honey Roll/Variations on Friends/Seasons/ Variations on Michelle's Song/Can I Put You On/Michelle's Song/I Meant To Do My Work Today (A Day In The Country)/Four Moods/Seasons (Reprise)

| **1971** | **Madman Across The Water** |

Tiny Dancer/Levon/Razor Face/Madman Across The Water/Indian Sunset/Holiday Inn/Rotten Peaches/All The Nasties/Goodbye

Year	Title
1972	**Honky Chateau**

Honky Cat/Mellow/I Think I'm Gonna Kill Myself/Suzie (Dramas)/Rocket Man (I Think It's Going To Be A Long Long Time)/Salvation /Slave/ Amy/Mona Lisas & Mad Hatters/Hercules

| **1973** | **Don't Shoot Me I'm Only The Piano Player** |

Daniel/Teacher I Need You/Elderberry Wine/Blues For My Baby And Me/Midnight Creeper/Have Mercy On The Criminal/I'm Gonna Be A Teenage Idol/Texan Love Song/Crocodile Rock/High Flying Bird

| **1973** | **Goodbye Yellow Brick Road** |

Funeral For A Friend/Love Lies Bleeding/Candle In The Wind/Bennie & The Jets/Goodbye Yellow Brick Road/This Song Has No Title/Grey Seal/Jamaica Jerk Off/I've Seen That Movie Too/Sweet Painted Lady/The Ballad Of Danny Bailey/Dirty Little Girl/All The Young Girls Love Alice/Your Sister Can't Twist (But She Can Rock & Roll)/Saturday Night's Alright For Fighting/Roy Rogers/Social Disease/Harmony

| **1974** | **Caribou** |

The Bitch Is Back/Pinky/Grimsby/Dixie Lily/Solar Prestige A Gammon/You're So Static/I've Seen The Saucers/Stinker/Don't Let The Sun Go Down On Me/ Ticking

| **1975** | **Captain Fantastic & The Brown Dirt Cowboy** |

Captain Fantastic & The Brown Dirt Cowboy/Tower Of Babel/Bitter Fingers/Tel Me When The Whistle Blows/Someone Saved My Life Tonight/(Gotta Get A) Meal Ticket/Better Off Dead/Writing/We All Fall In Love Sometimes/Curtains

Year	Title
1975	**Rock Of The Westies**

Medley (Yell Help; Wednesday Night: Ugly)/Dan Dare (Pilot Of The Future)/ Island Girl/Grow Some Funk Of Your Own/I Feel Like A Bullet (In The Gun Of Robert Ford)/Street Kids/Hard Luck Story/Feed Me/Billy Bones And The White Bird

Year	Title
1976	**Here & There**

Skyline Pigeon/Border Song/Honky Cat/Love Song/Crocodile Rock/Funeral For A Friend/Love Lies Bleeding/Rocket Man/Bennie & The Jets/Take Me To The Pilot

Year	Title
1976	**Blue Moves**

Your Starter For.../Tonight/One Horse Town/Chameleon/Boogie Pilgrim/Cage The Songbird/Crazy Water/Shoulder Holster/Sorry Seems To Be The Hardest Word/Out Of The Blue/Between Seventeen & Twenty/The Wide Eyed And Laughing/ Someone's Final Song/Where's The Shoorah/If There's A God In Heaven (What's He Waiting For ?)/Idol/Theme From A Non-Existent TV Series/Bite Your Lip (Get Up & Dance)

Year	Title
1978	**A Single Man**

Shine On Through/Return To Paradise/I Don't Care/Big Dipper/It Ain't Gonna Be Easy/Part-Time Love/Georgia/Shooting Star/Madness/Reverie/Song For Guy

Year	Title
1979	**Victim Of Love**

Johnny B.Goode/Warm Love In A Cold World/Born Bad/Thunder In The Night/ Spotlight/Street Boogie/Victim Of Love

Year	Title
1980	**21 At 33**

Chasing The Crown/Little Jeannie/Sartorial Eloquence/Two Rooms At The End Of The World/ White Lady White Powder/Dear God/Never Gonna Fall In Love Again/Take Me Back/Give Me The Love

Year	Title
1981	**The Fox**

Breaking Down The Barriers/Heart In The Right Place/Just Like Belgium/ Nobody Wins/Fascist Faces/Carla; Etude; Fanfare; Chloe/Heels Of The Wind/ Elton's Song/The Fox

Year	Title
1982	**Jump Up**

Dear John/Spiteful Child/Ball & Chain/Legal Boys/ I Am Your Robot/Blue Eyes/Empty Garden/ Princess/Where Have All The Good Times Gone/All Quiet On The Western Front

Year	Title
1983	**Too Low For Zero**

Cold As Christmas/I'm Still Standing/Too Low For Zero/Religion/I Guess That's Why They Call It The Blues/Crystal/Kiss The Bride/Whipping Boy/Saint/ One More Arrow

Year	Title
1984	**Breaking Hearts**

Restless/Slow Down Georgie (She's Poison)/Who Wears These Shoes ?/Breaking Hearts (Ain't What It Used To Be)/Li'l 'Frigerator/Passengers/In Neon/ Burning Buildings/Did He Shoot Her ?/Sad Songs (Say So Much)

Year	Title
1985	**Ice On Fire**

This Town/Cry To Heaven/Soul Glove/Nikita/Too Young/Wrap Her Up/Satellite/ Tell Me What The Papers Say/Candy By The Pound/Shoot Down The Moon/Act Of War

Album Discography

Year	Title
1986	**Leather Jackets**

Leather Jackets/Hoop Of Fire/Don't Trust That Woman/Go It Alone/Gypsy Heart/Slow Rivers/ Heartache All Over The World / Angeline /Memory Of Love/ Paris/I Fall Apart

Year	Title
1987	**Live In Australia**

Sixty Years On/I Need You To Turn To/The Greatest Discovery/Tonight/Sorry Seems To Be The Hardest Word/The King Must Die/Take Me To The Pilot/Tiny Dancer/Have Mercy On The Criminal/Madman Across The Water/Candle In The Wind/Burn Down The Mission/Your Song/Don't Let The Sun Go Down On Me

Year	Title
1988	**Reg Strikes Back**

Town Of Plenty/Word In Spanish/Mona Lisas And Mad Hatters (Part 2)/I Don't Wanna Go On With You Like That/Japanese Hands/Goodbye Marlon Brando/The Camera Never Lies/Heavy Traffic/Poor Cow/Since God Invented Girls

Year	Title
1989	**Sleeping With The Past**

Durban Deep/Healing Hands/Whispers/Club At The End Of The Street/Sleeping With The Past/Stones Throw From Hurtin'/Sacrifice/I Never Knew Her Name/ Amazes Me/Blue Avenue

Year	Title
1992	**The One**

Simple Life/The One/Sweat It Out/Runaway Train/Whitewash County/The North/ When A Woman Doesn't Want You/Emily/On Dark Street/Understanding Women/The Last Song

Year	Title
1993	**Duets**

Teardrops (with k.d.lang)/When I Think About Love (I Think About You) (with P.M.Dawn)/The Power (with Little Richard)/Shakey Ground (with Don Henley)/ True Love (with Kiki Dee)/If You Were Me (with Chris Rea)/A Woman's Needs (with Tammy Wynette)/Old Friend (with Nik Kershaw)/Go On And On (with Gladys Knight)/Don't Go Breaking My Heart (with RuPaul)/Ain't Nothing Like The Real Thing (with Marcella Detroit)/I'm Your Puppet(with Paul Young)/ Love Letters (with Bonnie Raitt)/Born To Lose (with Leonard Cohen)/Don't Let The Sun Go Down On Me (with George Michael)/Duets For One

Year	Title
1995	**The Lion King (soundtrack)**

I Just Can't Wait To Be King/Circle Of Life/Can You Feel The Love Tonight.
Other tracks on this album were performed by other artists.

Year	Title
1995	**Made In England**

Believe/Made In England /House /Cold /Pain/ Belfast/Latitude/Please/Man/Lies/ Blessed

A number of people whose assistance it is only right to acknowledge for the information they provided knowingly or otherwise: Mark Anders, Laura Beggs, Caroline Boucher, Julian Brown, Steve Brown, Dave Burland, Ann Cardew, Chris Charlesworth, B.J. Cole, David Costa, Dave Cousins, Tony Cousins, Dave Croker, Roger Dopson, Gus Dudgeon, Mike Evans, Alan Finch, Pete Frame, Alan Franks, Carolyn Hester, Mike Howard, Bill Levenson, Ralph & Nanna May, Bill McAllister, Wes McGhee, Crispin Murray, Philip Norman, Andy Peebles, Rocky Prior, Sir Tim Rice, Bridget St.John, Nick Stewart, Mike Storey, Laurent Thibault, Chris Thomas, Pete Thomas, Penny Valentine, Patty Vetta, Helen Walters, Jo Weinberg, Ray Williams, Brian Willoughby. Humble apologies to any whose names have inadvertently been omitted from this list. Special thanks to David Palmer who has so excellently designed this book. His approach is impressive and his taste (like my own) Olympian. David is a star. The various picture researchers who have worked on this project, especially Wendy Gay, Anna Smith and Claire Gouldstone, deserve credit for the material with which David has woven his magic.

My thanks to Michael Heatley, who more than helped out with the last two chapters, and to his faithful Sancho Panza, Ian Welch. This book is dedicated to Lynda Morrison, who put up with rather a lot during its gestation, but who greatly enjoyed the enforced diet of wall-to-wall Elton on the CD machine for many weeks. My mother's support is gratefully acknowledged - now 86 years old, she presumably realises that my getting a proper job is less and less likely - as is that of my children, Liz and Jane, my son-in-law, Simon, and my grandchildren, Joe, Jac, Isabel, Alex and Poppy. This book is also in memory of a beloved dog named Tiny Dancer, who went to canine heaven in the early 1980s.

John Tobler, 1995

Picture Acknowledgements

All Action 138, Jean Cummings 178.

Alpha 3c.m.r., 109, 198, 199, 201, Dave Benett 197, Alan Davidson 144, 151, Steve Finn 162 l., 192, Mark Mawson 203m.

Barnabys Picture Library 116 b.

Camera Press 168, Mark Anderson 169, T. Cooke 75m., 163b., Colin Davey 86 /87, Terry O'Neill 70/71, 75t., 82b., 90 /91, 90l., 91b.r., 93, 94l & r., 95t., 95m.l & m.r., 96 /97, 97m.,105,108, David White 82t

Colorific / Black Star Dennis Brack 43, 64.

Hulton Deutsch Collection 9, 13b., 50t.l., 52l., 54 /55, 65, 73, 76, 107, 111, 112, 113, 117b.,118t. 125.

Image Bank Nicholas Foster 94 background, David Jeffrey 26, Carlos Navajas 186 background Jeff Spielman 200.

Katz Stuart Nicol 119, Gerardo Somoza 190 l.

London Features International 3b.m.r., 44t., 56 m., 63, 98, 184b. r., 184t. r., Ross Barnett 154, Paul Cox 50b.m., S. Downie 183r., David Fisher 196, Alistair Linford 184b.l., Phil Loftus 184t.c.r., Kevin Mazur 3b.m.l., 3c.r., 166, 175, 183 l., 190r., 191, Philip Ollerenshaw 155r.,165, 173, Ken Reagan 184b.c.m., Ebet Roberts 56 l., Geoff Swaine 184b.c

Gary Merrin 3c.l., 3c.m.l., 36 l., 37, 156, 158.

Pictorial Press 12, 13t., 14, 77, 161, 162r., 163m., Bob Gruen 74t., van Houten 85, Jeffrey Mayer 3b.l., 3b. r., 44b., 99,131, 135, 148, Rob Verhorst 128/129, 132, Vinnie Zuffante 140.

Barry Plummer 18, 19 l., 22, 24, 25m., 25t., 27 b.l., 28, 45, 51, 53, 57 background, 57 l., 67, 80 l., 80t.r., 81, 89b., 118m.

Range Pictures Ltd /Bettmann 20, 89 t.

Redferns 10, 123 l., Richie Aaron 3t.m.r., David Redfern 33m., Ian Dickson 47, D. Ellis 3t.m.l., 38, Gems 21r., Fraser Gray 3t.l., Mick Hutson 184t.c.m., 186m., Ian Dickson 184b.m., Bob King 149, 155 l., Neil Lange 184b.c.l., Lorne Resnick 184t.l., Mike Prior 121, R.B. 30 /31, 21 l., 25b.; Ebet Roberts 136, 164, 170, Peter Sanders 33 l., Jim Steele 184t.c.l., Val Wilmer 6, 27r., Graham Wiltshire 194.

Relay Photos Ltd A.Byrne 23, 34, 52r., Andre Csillag 142, 171, Chris Walker 95b., 124.

Retna 58 /59, 60, 61m., 61r., 61 l., Ross Barnett 143 t., Adrian Boot 62, Ross Marino 3t.r., 153, Photofest 104., Michael Putland 19r., 27m., 32, 36m & r., 42, 46, 58m., 58 /59, 79, 80 b., 123r., Steve Rapport 141t., 181, Jodi Summers 137, Ed Sykes 184t.m., Timothy White 143b.

Rex Features 35, 139, 141b., 163t., David Dagley 4, 102 /103, Frank Edwards 78, Eugene Adebari 180.

The Salvation Army 15.

Scope Features 74 b., 122.

S.I.N David Corio 115, U.Natola 162t, Peter Noble 120.

Sotheby's / Harvey Goldsmith Entertainment Ltd 117t.

Frank Spooner Pictures 195, Alain Ben 179.

Tony Stone Images Ric Ergenbright 203 background, Ed Pritchard 116 background.

Laurent Thibault 48, 49.